PRAISE FOR

ROCK STAR
Adjacent

"Art's journey in the music industry is a rollercoaster of experiences, from the highs of success to the lows of self-discovery. It's a reminder that life, like music, is a beautiful composition of lessons. Having navigated the actor's side of the industry myself and having slept many a night on Art's couch and he on mine, I can attest to the truth he speaks. Proud of my brother."

Ricardo A. Chavira, Actor Known for *Desperate Housewives*, *Selena: The Series* (Netflix), and *Truth Be Told*

"Art is a well-seasoned road warrior with vast experience . . . and experiences. *Rock Star Adjacent* gives firsthand accounts of the whacky and wonderful world of rock star touring that will keep you enthralled. A great read!"

Steve Jensen, Artist Manager for Artists including k.d. lang and Katy Perry

"Art gives readers a triple A (access all areas) backstage pass to his life both in and out of the music business. The tours, legends, and behind-the-scenes stories are great, but his personal gains and setbacks on the road to self-discovery are the heart of this book."

Kathy Valentine, Author, Songwriter, and Bassist for The Go-Go's

"Patrick Stansfield taught Art well. Not only has he become a top Tour Manager to some of the biggest artists on the planet, but he has that unmistakable knack for telling a great story just like our most revered mentor did for so many years. Patrick is looking down very proud of all the accomplishments Art has made, and this book is right up there with some of Art's biggest. A definite read for anyone who wants to know what it's really like 'on the road.'"

Brian Crouch, Tour Manager for Artists including The Goo Goo Dolls, My Chemical Romance, The Offspring, Michelle Branch, and Morrissey

"Art is a talented, thoughtful, and caring human being. He helped me immensely in a very difficult time; shepherding the band in my absence. I am most grateful to have him as a friend. And like anyone who has done what we do for a period of time, he has some good stories too!"

Lol Halsey, Tour Manager for Huey Lewis and the News

STORIES FROM THE ROAD

ROCK STAR
Adjacent

FORMER CONCERT TOUR MANAGER
ARTURO CISNEROS

Paperback ISBN: 979-8-9892121-1-8
eBook ISBN: 979-8-9892121-0-1

BIO008000 BIOGRAPHY & AUTOBIOGRAPHY / Music
BIO005000 BIOGRAPHY & AUTOBIOGRAPHY / Entertainment & Performing Arts
BIO026000 BIOGRAPHY & AUTOBIOGRAPHY / Personal Memoirs

Cover design and typesetting by Kaitlin Barwick
Cover photo by Priscilla Du Preez on Unsplash
Edited by Justin Greer, Valene Wood, and Deborah Spencer

www.rockstaradjacent.com
www.psa-entertainment.com

I dedicate this book to my mama.

Thank you for encouraging me to travel, to explore what the world has to offer, and to never stop learning.

Dedico este libro a mi mamá.

Gracias por animarme a viajar, explorar lo que el mundo tiene para ofrecer, y nunca dejar de aprender.

Mom (El Paso, 2022)

Thank you for purchasing my book.
A portion of the royalties from this book will be donated
to support the nonprofit organization Mija, Yes You Can®,
which is based in my hometown of El Paso, Texas.

Mija, Yes You Can®
Mission Statement

"We empower and advocate for women of all ages, races,
ethnicities, social-economic status, sexual and gender
identities to achieve gender equality in all aspects of life.
We aim to provide resources and education to women and
girls in order to help them achieve their ambitions in life."

www.mijayesyoucan.org

Mija, Yes You Can® was not involved
in the creation of this book.

Contents

CONTENTS

From the Author

When I was traveling extensively as a concert tour/road manager (going to various parts of the world—53 countries so far), many of my friends and family members always asked if I needed an assistant or if they could jump into my suitcase so they could tag along. This was the running joke because they were in awe at the amazing travel opportunities my career afforded me. Yes, I agree—I have been very lucky to travel all over the world and take in some amazing views and experience various cultures—but I also see the personal growth and transformation all this traveling has given me. It's true when they say, the best education is in traveling.

I invite you to join me on the journey of my life as I revisit some of the memories from the past, ponder on the future, and take in the present. Along the way I'll share some of the lessons I've learned and some of the lessons and knowledge imparted to me by my mentor, Patrick "Paddy" Stansfield. I'll share Paddy's "lessons from the road" distilled into words that I simply referred to as "Paddyisms." The Paddyisms are quotes he shared with us, and I do not attribute Patrick as the author of the quotes, simply the educator sharing them.

I'm not here to speak with any authority, but to simply share my lived experiences. I leave it up to you, the reader, to take what you find useful and to leave behind what you don't. Feel free to laugh along, be sad, or ponder for bit, and hopefully view things from a different perspective with hopes of finding some enlightenment you seek in your own journey. The stories you will soon read are in no order; consider them little vignettes from my time on the road, collected here to offer some life lessons.

My journey began in my hometown of El Paso, Texas. Starting from working in my parent's grocery store and moving on through working my way up to management in the hotel industry, being an actor on stage and TV commercials, and then transitioning into the music industry by managing concert tours around the world. This led to managing artists and producing an award-winning documentary, and ultimately writing this book.

En route, I've been challenged with my own acceptance of my sexuality, coming out, isolation, depression, anxiety, loneliness, feeling that I wasn't enough, and even thoughts of ending it all. But somehow, I've managed to find the strength to continue this journey of mine, to see how my story ends.

And I'm not finished yet.

You don't have to sneak along in my suitcase—I'm inviting you as my guest. Let's pack up and get ready to embark on this adventure.

Arturo

On the tour bus driving into Washington, DC
(Manilow Tour 2004)

1

Road Life

L et me give you a small glimpse of the road life I've experienced.

Managing an artist and their concert tour isn't easy, but it is very rewarding. Here is a quick background of the people involved in a concert tour. You first have the tour manager, who is the main person looking after everything and everyone, including the artist. The size of the tour will dictate how many responsibilities they will have. Smaller tours with very little budget will likely require people to do double duty, while the larger arena/stadium tours will have an army of personnel to split up those responsibilities. Next you have a production manager; they will generally oversee all the production of the show (the building of the show) and managing the crews. Some tours will have tour accountants who keep tabs on the budget and all expenses on the road and will work with the promoters to settle the show (determining the financials of each show). On some tours I handled this as tour manager. Then there are production designers who work with the artist to develop the look of the show (everything from set pieces to innovative ideas). They work hand in hand with lighting designers to create the lighting vision and utilize new technology to give the audience the eye candy they seek along with great music. Then there are various sound and lighting crews (who work to set up the gear to execute the sound and lighting). Carpenters who build the stage, riggers who hang and secure the equipment above everyone, security who travel with the tour overseeing the safety of the artist throughout the entire day and securing the venue as well. Then of course you have the bus and truck drivers, and if it's a large arena tour, there might also be a catering crew that travels with the group, preparing all show-day meals for everyone.

Behind the scenes (those who are usually not out on the road) you have business managers who pay the bills, work with the tour accountant or tour manager to keep track of expenses, and many other financial matters. And finally, you have managers, or personal managers as they are sometimes referred to, who guide the career of the artist; they work with the booking agent to book the venues and what cities to go to and when. They also work with promoters and publicists to get the word out about the tour and ensure tickets sell. They do a lot more behind the scenes that many people don't usually know about or see, but along with tour managers, they are the "make it happen" folks.

Okay, that's the background on touring . . . now some of the ups and downs of touring.

The upside is that you get to travel all over the world. Some tours are just domestic in their respective countries, and others are international; it depends on the artist and their popularity. I've been fortunate to work with artists whose tours have taken me around the world. The downside of all this travel is that many times you are moving every other day from city to city and at times it doesn't give you time to see anything in the city, but then again, you aren't on vacation, you are there to work! But we all find ways to squeeze in some fun.

For example, I've been fortunate to taste some rare, very expensive wines in Australia and the United Kingdom. I've met the duke of Marlborough when we did a show at Blenheim Palace with Barry Manilow, as well as the duke of Bedford on several visits to Woburn Abbey with Neil Diamond; and, on both occasions, I have taken private tours of both places. Along with meeting various other celebrities, I've been introduced to some of the finest foods and experiences in life. I've had friends in similar positions meet the pope, presidents, queens, and many other dignitaries from around the world.

The constant move is exhausting. Even though you might be staying in nice hotels, you are constantly living out of your luggage and checking in and out of said hotels. If you travel by tour bus, then sometimes you sleep on the bus. These are very luxurious, million-plus-dollar buses and I must say the ride is pretty comfy. Sometimes I prefer not checking into a hotel and just staying on the bus! Then there are those who fly on private jets from city to city, and I've done that too. It is a bit easier and does offer more time in a city, allowing you get there quicker so you have more opportunities to squeeze in some fun.

Another upside is that all your travel expenses are covered. Though you're responsible for your own meals on no-show days, you do get to save a lot of money because a majority of everything is covered by the tour. That's a big plus for many folks in this line of work.

The downside of traveling is not being home, and that can cause a big problem in the family/love relationship category. I've seen many divorces and breakups, but I've equally seen many successful long-term marriages and relationships do just fine. It is tough, and missing out on your kids' lives can be hard down the road.

Between tours when everyone goes home, just think of what someone with a family must go through to reintegrate themselves back into family life. From not being present for daily events to suddenly being there can throw the household routine off.

For a single person like me, it was a big challenge as well. I would go from being surrounded by hundreds of people to just being by myself once I got back home. Talk about going from hot to cold! There were times that it didn't affect me; but other times, it was mentally draining and challenging. The emptiness of my home would thicken the sense of isolation, and the depression would grow like quick spreading mold, making everything dark and gloomy. Yes, I had a network of friends, but that sometimes didn't correct the situation. Some of those friends' lives had moved on and continued to grow without me around so sometimes it was just playing catch-up with friends, until suddenly it was time to go on tour again for another varying amount of time.

Depending on the tour, I could be gone for weeks or even months at a time without returning home. Presently I still deal with some residual effects. I no longer can work all day at home; I must go somewhere to be surrounded by people. Coffee shops are my remote office.

Traveling can sometimes play tricks with your mind. You'll start forgetting what date/day it is. On many occasions I've woken up in a panic in a hotel room wondering where I was, where I was supposed to be, and if I was late. On a few occasions I've called the hotel operator and politely yet with some sense of urgent confusion asked where I was, the city, state, and hotel name, and what day of the week and date it was! Of course, I always began with, "Please don't laugh or be frightened," then I asked the awkward question. It usually brings out a giggle, and I too giggle so that they know I'm not someone who has lost his mind. I then grab my tour itinerary and find that date and usually see it's a day off! Well, we don't really have days off, but it's not a show day at least. Yeah, that's a crazy feeling to go through and unfortunately, I've experienced it once too many times.

Traveling all over the world has brought me in front of many people from various cultures and backgrounds, and because of that I feel more compassion for the differences in people and cultures. That to me is the beauty of traveling. I'm sure you have heard the expression "traveling educates," because it does. You get to deal with many people from various backgrounds who speak various languages. Part of the beauty of it too is that not everyone speaks English! I've had to learn some key phrases in other languages so that I could do my job. But more important, so that I might be able to communicate and co-mingle with the people of whatever country I'm traveling through.

You also get to eat amazing foods from different cultures and countries and learn about some of their traditions and history. My life has been enriched because of this. To this date I have friends all over the world who I keep in touch with. I know that if I ever make it back to their country, I'll be welcomed with open arms and will have someone to sit down with to enjoy a nice meal and conversation, something I have done on several occasions!

This leads me to the touring family you build while touring with so many people day in and out for an extended period. There is a bond that you can't describe, but it's one that is so strong it lasts for many years to come. After a tour ends, you hope to see them down the road and when you do, it's like you just saw them the day before, without skipping a beat.

MY BIRTHDAY IN LONDON

One year I was fortunate to celebrate my birthday in London after the United Kingdom portion of the tour ended (I think it was my 40th). As luck would have it, the tour was scheduled to end on July 28, and everyone was scheduled to fly to his/her respective home city on July 29—my birthday.

I knew this was happening well in advance when I received the touring schedule and had to begin arranging all the logistics for the tour. Well, I wasn't planning on spending my birthday sitting on a flight from London to Los Angeles, that was for sure, so I had to have a plan B set up for when I would let the artist know what was happening and ensure he was okay with me not traveling back with the group. As road manager, it was my job to travel with the artist party to ensure everything went smoothly and I was there to handle things if needed.

I had a few colleagues who knew it was my birthday and we all coordinated our schedules to stay over and spend a few days extra exploring London and celebrating my birthday. Many times, when a tour includes another country and is ending there or taking a break for a while, some people like to take advantage of the fact that the return flight is already covered by the tour and sometimes extend their return and make a vacation out of it.

I had to plan the timing of when I would discuss my birthday plans with the artist, because, as I said earlier, it would mean he would not have me traveling with him if something needed fixing. When the time was right, I brought it up to the artist and he was in total agreement with me staying over and celebrating my birthday and making some great memories. He even went a step further and told me to put the extra hotel nights on his tab and to add a nice birthday dinner on to that as well; what a great guy!

Since I was the one who booked the hotel for the tour, I had already mentioned to the hotel my desire to stay over a few extra nights; I just needed to give them the green light once I knew it was going to happen. The hotel surprised me with a nice bottle of champagne and a two-hour massage treatment, so that I could get my birthday celebration off to a good start.

Once the group was gone, my colleagues and I set out to visit Windsor Castle and explore London and its many wonderful pubs and restaurants. They even decided to handcuff me to a railing in Hyde Park! (Check out the picture.)

This birthday is one I often think of fondly, and it always brings a smile to my face.

Hancuffed in Hyde Park (London, 2008)

2

Fulfilling a Promise Led Me to My Career

In the summer of 1997, I drove from Dallas, Texas, to Los Angeles, California, (LA) to get my formal training as an actor. I was 30 years old and instead of being deep in a career, I was finally pursuing my dream of being in the entertainment business. On the advice of my talent agent in Dallas, I auditioned for The American Academy of Dramatic Arts to be accepted into their summer program. They auditioned over 4000 people across the country and only accepted 400 and I was fortunate to be one of them. I had a choice between LA or New York City and chose LA. That entire summer I would be emersed in classes of dance, movement, voice, Shakespeare, and of course acting!

After finishing up my studies at The American Academy of Dramatic Arts in LA, I was successful in securing a talent agent quickly. I was fortunate to sign on with one of the top agencies in LA at that time, (Sutton, Barth & Vennari), and began auditioning and booking TV commercials.

After about a year of this, I realized that I was going to stay in LA permanently and knew I would do whatever it took to stay and make a living. Los Angeles was going to be my home. With that being decided, it was time to fulfill a promise I had made to my mom before I left home, and that was to go through the confirmation process with the Catholic church. I was the only member of my family of 9 children that didn't do that as a youth. For some reason I fell through the cracks and my mom had always felt bad about that; so, I promised her that once I found my new home city, I would do it. I reached out to my local church and signed up for the classes. (Just so you know, it takes about 6–8 weeks of classes studying the Bible and learning about the religion before I can fully be confirmed in a religious ceremony.) I started my classes and halfway through them, I was already getting tired of the commercial acting business. I was also very frustrated that I couldn't break into the theatrical (TV/film) side of the business. I wanted more from life, and my part-time job and chasing the acting career wasn't cutting it for me, even though I was doing pretty good at the acting work.

One day at confirmation class, I sat behind a guy that was wearing a Luis Miguel jacket. Luis Miguel is a big Latin artist that many have referred to as the Frank Sinatra of Latin music. Anyway, the guy I was sitting behind was a white guy and I mention this because I found it odd that this white guy would be wearing a jacket you'd buy at a concert of a Latin artist. Well, during our break, I walked up to him and inquired about the jacket and asked if he listened to that music. I was just honest with the confusion and curiosity of it all. He laughed and educated me on the fact that the jacket was a touring jacket, a gift to all the crew and band working on the concert tour. It's called SWAG (Stuff We All Get). On the front upper shoulder area, it was embroidered with the word "CREW" on it. He was an audio engineer on the tour. We got to talking and he filled me in on what a tour was and everything it entailed. I was blown away with it all. I never really gave it much thought as to the amount of people working behind the scenes of a concert. I guess I just thought the show just popped up one evening . . . lol. I mentioned to him my situation and the fact that I was becoming bored with the acting work and wouldn't mind finding a new line of work. After I informed him that I had six years of hotel management experience behind me, he suggested I contact his management because they could probably use my hotel experience with the tour. The following week he brought his tour itinerary, a book that is made for everyone on the tour that contains all the daily details of the tour: each city, hotel, movement, show info, and so on. It also lists of the names and contact information for all management. I copied down the name of the business manager and figured I would reach out.

Over the next few days, I decided to work on my résumé and make it more business oriented with all my past experiences. Then I decided to call the business manager and, to my surprise, I was able to get the assistant to connect me to the business manager directly. While I stated my case, she was so kind and listened to everything I had to say. Then she mentioned she too was originally from Texas, Lubbock to be exact! Well, that broke down a wall. She suggested I contact the tour manager and inquire with him if he would be able to use my services. She mentioned she would also reach out to him to give him a heads up. She then instructed her assistant to give me the contact information for the tour manager so that I could reach out. I was blown away at everything that was happening and, knowing what I know now about the business, I realize how fortunate I was that she showed me such rare kindness.

The next day I called the tour manager, Tom Mooney. He was very gruff with me and questioned how I got his number and, after grilling me for a bit, he suggested I fax him my résumé so he could review it and get back to me. But before he hung up, he asked me once again who exactly gave me his number and referred to the assistant by a different name. I corrected him and said her real name, and he then came back with, "I know that's her name, I just wanted to make sure you weren't bullshitting me," and hung up. After that call I thought, *This guy is an asshole!* And I questioned if I wanted to pursue this; but I was still very intrigued at the idea of working on a tour, so I sent in my résumé and hoped for the best.

The next day he called and asked me to come to his home for a meeting, since he worked out of his home rather than an office building. I later found out almost everyone in the touring industry does so, and I would too for the rest of my career. I agreed and drove out to his home in Encino. As I pulled up, I sat in my '92 Saturn and stared at his huge house and all the other huge homes on his block. I couldn't believe I was about to enter such a big and beautiful home. I buzzed the gate, and he asked me to park on the street and walk into the yard, and he would meet me there. Out came this tall man with a mustache and a strong Boston accent and, I would later find out, an Irishman too! We exchanged hellos and after he looked over his flower beds and checked on his prize flowers, he led me into his home and into his home office.

We sat there and talked for a good while. Then the phone rang, and he excused himself while he answered the call. He explained that he was expecting an important call from a promoter in Spain, and he didn't want to miss it. I sat there as he went back and forth with the promoter speaking slow, which I figured was probably because the person on the other end didn't speak English too well and I was correct; they were having a bit of a language issue. He put the call on hold, took a breather, and asked me to wait a bit longer so he could finish the call and then we could finish our meeting. I asked him if I could help; since I spoke fluent Spanish, I could probably bridge the language gap and solve whatever it was they were having problems with. He took the call off hold and handed me the receiver. I introduced myself (in Spanish) to the man on the other end and I heard a big sigh of relief come from his end. He was happy to hear my Spanish and immediately jumped into explaining to me what he was trying to convey to the tour manager, which I, in turn, translated to the tour manager, who was now smiling. This went on for a few minutes as I went back and forth until the issue was resolved, and everyone was satisfied.

After the call, the tour manager looked at me, said, "I could use you," and offered me an internship. "Yeah, no thanks," I said, "I don't work for free." He laughed and said, "Okay." Then he said he would review the budget to see what he could pay me and that he would call me the following day. When he did call me the next morning, he mentioned a salary amount which was way more than I was making as an actor and my part-time job. Just as I was about to accept the offer, he clarified the salary amount was a weekly figure. I had assumed it was a monthly figure. Wow, I couldn't believe it! Of course, without hesitation, I accepted the job. I was going to get paid that much plus my traveling expenses were being covered and I was going to go to Spain for a full month!

I stood my ground and recognized my value; I wasn't going to work for free! This not only got me a great salary, but it also won Tom's respect for me for doing so.

This is where it all began, my career in the music industry working with rockstar legends and industry giants. Keeping my word has always been something I've prided myself on and, although there have been times where I wasn't able to (due to various reasons), I always strived to do so. When I started the Catholic confirmation classes, I had no idea this was about to happen to me, and who I was meeting and would meet. I was just keeping a promise, and because of that, it put me in a place and time where I would have the opportunity to inquire about a job, and all that put me on a path that would change my life. Tom was best friends with Doug Pope, who was the production manager on the tour he hired me for, and they both were best friends with Patrick Stansfield. Patrick was a giant in the industry and worked with Neil Diamond for over 25 years, among many, many other legends and icons. These three men were very influential in my career and were always there to guide me. I always admired how they got along and treated each other and especially how they would refer to each other. On many occasions they would refer to each other as "dear," as in "hello, dear," "good-bye, dear," and so on. Their friendship was something very special to witness. I'm glad I was part of that.

Paddyism

"Don't shirk responsibility.
Don't accept responsibility without authority.
Don't accept authority without compensation."

3

My First Trip Overseas

In 1998 I was new to the business of touring and on my first trip overseas in Spain. I was there months before the tour would start, and the purpose of my trip was to advance the hotels and logistics in each city prior to the tour's arrival. I had to see for myself the conditions of the hotel and rooms to ensure they were up to the artist's standards.

This was my first trip out of the country; I didn't even have a passport or luggage! Tom took me to an outlet store just outside of Los Angeles to purchase proper touring luggage. I then had to maneuver my way through obtaining an expedited passport, a first for me dealing with the federal government, but not the last. I became very well versed in all the dealings with passport renewals and visas as my career progressed. I also had to obtain an international driver's license because I was going to have to drive while in Spain. I was a bit nervous about that. Come to think of it, I was nervous about the entire trip. Again, it was my first trip out of the country, and I was being entrusted with so much so fast. Have you ever heard of the imposter syndrome? In short, it's when you doubt your skills, talents, or accomplishments and have this fear that you'll be exposed as a fraud. That's part of what I was dealing with. I just had to believe in myself, rely on my past managerial experience, and deal with everything with a sense of practicality.

During this trip I was in the city of Gijon, which is on the central-northern part of Spain, about a five-hour drive from Madrid. While there looking at hotels, I was informed by the promoter that the type of Mercedes the artist had requested was not available in that city but that he had an alternate option. I didn't feel good about this alternate option, so I asked him to arrange for the vehicle to be brought to my hotel to inspect. He agreed and that afternoon I got a call from the front desk informing me there was someone to see me; I recognized the name as the person who was supposed to bring the vehicle. I made my way down to the front desk and met the man as he escorted me to the front drive where the vehicle was parked. As I exited the hotel, I quickly caught a glimpse of an older, brown model Mercedes-Benz. It was easily identifiable as an older model, and the brown color was hard to miss. My instincts were right, this alternate option the promoter had was not going to work. I was courteous and thanked the man for bringing the vehicle to me and informed him I would discuss it with the promoter.

As I turned to go back inside the hotel, I could see the look on the doorman's face. His expression said exactly what I was thinking; I knew I had to find something better. I quickly called the promoter in Madrid to discuss my disappointment with the vehicle. That was when he informed me that this brown vehicle was the only local option, otherwise he would have to drive an acceptable one up from Madrid and that was going to be costly.

On my way out to dinner that evening, I saw the same doorman and struck up a conversation with him about the brown Mercedes I had seen earlier. He was curious as to why I was looking at it. I informed him why and that it needed to be that specific model (the newest model I could find—preferably a brand new one) and in the color black. He then told me his brother-in-law had that exact model, brand new and in black! I said, "That's nice, but would he rent it out to us?"

He said, "I'm sure he would," and offered to make a call. I couldn't believe what I was hearing! That's when I told him I was leaving the next day and if he could get an answer for me sooner rather than later that would be great!

While I was having dinner, my cell phone rang and it was the doorman; his brother-in-law was willing to rent us his Mercedes and would drive it himself. This was amazing! I asked him for his brother-in-law's information and quickly called him and discussed seeing the car in person the morning before I left. He agreed.

I then called the promoter and informed him what I had discovered, and he was quick to want to dismiss it, but I reminded him how particular the artist was, and that the artist would not ride in the brown one and driving one from Madrid was a waste of money when we already had one locally. I informed him I was going to see it the next morning and would call him with my final verdict.

My next call was to Tom, the tour manager (my boss), to fill him in on the developments. He was quick to agree with my suggestion and said he would speak directly with the promoter to ensure he understood that if I approved the vehicle, it would be up to him (the promoter) to secure that vehicle and ensure it was the one that would be used for the artist.

The next morning before I drove out of the city, the doorman's brother-in-law was in front of the hotel waiting for me. I met with him and inspected the vehicle and immediately knew that it would be perfect. I informed the promoter and left the details to him to work out with the owner of the car.

Tom was very pleased with everything I had arranged, and he was particularly happy that the car was just what the artist wanted and liked. The artist never really knew the challenge we had in getting the vehicle, but the fact that he was happy, and didn't skip a beat over the vehicle he was riding in, made me feel happy with my work. Our job is making things happen and making it look like it's a normal thing in everyday life, even though many times it's not.

It's crazy how some things work out. A casual conversation and being nice led to the doorman of the hotel helping me find the solution to our Mercedes-Benz problem. Over the years of being in this industry, I'm still struck with astonishment when I see people treating others like they are below them and even treating them with a dismissive attitude. I'm of the mind that once I put someone on a pedestal, I automatically position myself on a different level from them. I believe that simply showing respect and kindness to others encourages the same in return, placing each of us on the same level. And sometimes that encourages the desire to simply help someone for no other reason than to know we've helped another human being.

Paddyism

"It's our relationships with people that will keep us off the bread line."

Art in Spain (Spain, 1998)

4

Life-Work Balance
Moderation

I thought I was having a heart attack and fell to the
ground. He offered to pop my back and had his chiropractor come back and work on me.

All this as he was making his way to the stage to start
his concert!

Allow me to elaborate. While on tour, the stress builds
up. I'm constantly moving from city to city, sometimes on
a tour bus that feels like a submarine on wheels along with
10–12 fellow tour mates and everything that comes along
with living in tight quarters. On top of that I have my workload and all the responsibilities that come with that. So, I
either work out to let it go or hit the bar to drown it out, or
something else to find the means of releasing the stress so
that it doesn't build up. On this particular tour I was very
busy and, as much as I like to work out, I couldn't fit in the
time as much as I wanted. This led to what transpired one
evening just as the show was about to begin.

I was in the touring production office at the arena doing
my work. On this tour I wasn't directly involved with getting the artist to stage so I would just sit in the office and get

work done during the show. This particular evening, as I was working in the office all alone, I hit print on my laptop. As the paper came out of the printer (which was conveniently placed within arm's reach), I reached over to grab it. At that moment I felt this squeeze in my chest area. It was so painful and powerful that I fell to the ground next to my chair. I tried gasping for air, but it was difficult to do so. It felt as if someone was squeezing my heart and sucking all the air out of my lungs.

As I was on the floor gripping my chest, I realized that the show was starting, and nobody would be back into the office for about another 15–20 minutes. I knew I needed to get help, but I couldn't reach for my radio that was sitting on the table, because any upward movement was extremely painful. That's when I realized I was better off crawling to the door and flagging someone down for help. I crawled to the door and just as I opened it, security was walking by with the artist headed to the stage. They all looked down and saw me and immediately noticed something was wrong. I was scooped up by security and could hear the artist tell them to take me to his dressing room and to call the doctor.

When I was finally able to catch my breath and explained where the pain was coming from, the artist commented that it was most likely my back and instructed someone to call the chiropractor back if she hadn't left the building yet. This artist usually had a chiropractor work on him before the show, so I was lucky the chiropractor was nearby. All this time, the show obviously had not started since the artist was there. That's when the tour manager said it was best that he started the show and that they would look after me to ensure I was okay.

Once the chiropractor arrived, she quickly figured out it was my back that had locked, and she was going to have to do her magic to unlock it. She warned me it was going to be both painful yet relieving; her magic brought tears to my eyes for both reasons too. After several adjustments and a massage, she instructed me to relax and not move around too much. I would have to do a follow-up in the next city with another chiropractor to ensure it would not lock up again.

It goes without saying that this was a wakeup call for me. Although it turned out to be my back locking up because of stress, it felt like a heart attack, and that scared me. The lesson I took from this was that I needed to work on reducing my stress and taking better care of myself.

After this tour, I was exhausted and, once I got back home to Los Angeles, I was on a call with my travel agent and friend Edie and she commented on how tired I sounded. I agreed and filled her in on the stress I had dealt with on tour and my medical incident. At this point she commented that I needed a vacation to relax and recharge. Again, I agreed with my wise friend as she proceeded to tell me she was going to book a vacation for me for the coming week. I didn't have anything on my calendar for the next three weeks so I gave her the green light.

Within a few days I was approving my vacation trip to the Grand Caymans. I had never been there and although I wasn't a beach person, the white sandy beaches and crystal blue warm waters were like nothing I had seen before and definitely not what we have here in California!

While there, I didn't schedule anything. I would just wake up and then proceed to explore and go with the flow. It was during this trip that I began my journey of being more mindful and what would later become my lifelong search for life-work balance, or as I prefer to call it, life-work moderation, because I believe it's more of a moderation thing than a balance thing.

It started with the most out-of-nowhere experience with the cocktail waitress. I was lounging at the pool reading when the waitress came over to take my order. I ordered an iced tea and she looked at me and said, "TEA?" Then she asked if I was on vacation and proceeded to inform me that the pool had a swim-up bar and that it was open! It was 11:00 a.m. and I was on vacation, so why was I ordering a tea when what I really wanted was a stereotypical tropical drink to kick off my vacation? I asked her to bring me one and she gave me a big smile of approval and a "hell yeah!"

When she returned with my drink, she caught me looking at my watch and here is where she unknowingly tossed the pebble of wisdom into my brain's pond of knowledge and began the ripples of curiosity that continue to this day to deliver insightful thoughts. She asked if I had an appointment or somewhere I needed to be. After answering no and explaining that looking at my watch is just a habit, she reminded me I was on vacation and that the island life is relaxed and easy going and she suggested I take off my watch for the entire duration of my stay and not be a slave to time.

I looked at her and took in the wise words and simply said, "You are right, I will." And I did. To this date, I do not wear a watch.

Gay Hendricks has a great chapter about time in his book *The Big Leap: Conquer Your Hidden Fear and Take Life to the Next Level* that I would recommend. In his book he writes about the difference between the Newtonian Time paradigm and the Einstein Time paradigm. One of my takeaways from that book is that we allow time to own us and control us, when it's us who create time and own it. My mindset changed and I began to work at not rushing to catch up to time or to make up for time. I valued how I used my time. The same goes for phones; I began to not jump every time my phone rang and being okay with missed calls going to voicemail. I wasn't going to be a slave to my phone either.

The rest of my vacation was filled with me wandering around on long walks, taking excursions, swimming with stingrays, snorkeling, and just being in the moment.

This more relaxed attitude is probably why I was able to enjoy myself more and welcomed connections and conversations with everyone I met. As a matter of fact, this is probably why I was mentally available to meeting this guy who was vacationing alone from London. He was an attorney and we met at the bar one evening. It was a Texas-themed bar/restaurant that was owned by a former Texan—yeah, small world. We chatted over drinks and mingled with various people throughout the evening. At the end of the evening, we both were pretty drunk and it so happened that his hotel was next to mine so we decided to walk together in the darkness, stumbling along the way and finally arriving at my hotel first. This is where I was surprised when he suggested having a nightcap in my room. I was up for one more drink—why not?

As we entered my room it *finally* hit me what was happening and although we never discussed either one of us being into guys, somehow, he just took a wild guess and let's just say it was great he did. Boy, this vacation was doing wonders for me.

NO GOOD DEED GOES UNPUNISHED

After I arrived back home in LA from my vacation, I got a call from an old friend named Sergio to invite me out for beers and a few games of darts. We both enjoyed playing darts, so I accepted. We decided on an Irish pub near my place and met up there. While there we met two girls playing darts and played several games with them until closing time. After settling our tab and as the lights came on giving everyone the cue to leave, we said our good-byes to the girls and began to head out the door with all the remaining patrons.

At this time my friend was talking to someone outside. As I waited on him to finish, I noticed one of the girls we were playing with came out and was about to turn the corner of the building when some guy hugs her from behind and kisses her on the cheek. I thought nothing of it, until she yelled at him to get away and questioned his actions. I

27

figured he was probably drunk and making an aggressive pass at her. She saw me so I decided to walk up to her to see if she was okay. She told me she didn't know the guy and didn't want him touching her. At this point the guy in question began to try and sweet-talk her. I interrupted him and asked him to leave her alone, pointing out the fact that she had stated she didn't know him nor desired any of his advances. I turned to get my friend's attention and as I turned back, I received a sucker punch in the face. I immediately dropped down to the floor. Now the center of attention, people began to scatter as my friend made his way over to me. Two other guys (friends of the guy who hit me) jumped out from the bushes and a full-on fight broke out, three of them against my friend and me.

I got thrown into the busy street and by sheer luck didn't get hit by any oncoming traffic. After I tried to stop the instigator several times, the bartender came out, grabbed and dragged me into the bar, and instructed my friend to follow. Then he closed and locked the door once he had us safely inside. I was bleeding from my nose, mouth, and an open wound on my head, and I was feeling severe pain in my ribs and back. My friend had a big gash on his head and was also bleeding. The girl was nowhere to be found; she got in her car and left.

Someone must have called the police as soon as the fight started because they arrived quickly and were able to apprehend the main guy that started the fight. However, the officers threatened to arrest me as well if I was going to press charges on the guy, because, as they put it, he could press charges on me as well.

At this point I was mentally out of it and was dealing with all my injuries, so my thinking was not too good. I agreed not to press charges out of fear of being arrested myself, so the police let all parties leave. My friend took me home to mend my wounds.

The next morning, the pain was worse, and I discovered my two front teeth were broken and my jaw was swollen and in severe pain. I called my dentist to been seen immediately, and he agreed. I had my friend drive me to his office, because I was in too much pain to concentrate on driving. The first thing he did was take an X-ray and it revealed my jaw had been broken and I was going to need surgery to repair it. The broken teeth would have to wait since the jaw took priority. He called in a favor with an oral surgeon friend of his to see if he could see me immediately, which, lucky for me, he was able to. I then had my roommate drive me over to the oral surgeon's office a few miles away.

Things moved fast here. I went into the oral surgeon's office to discover the severity of my jaw and sure enough I needed immediate surgery because my jaw was almost detached. It just so happened that his office was not far from the hospital he worked out of, so I decided to have my roommate drive me over to get admitted for the surgery. Hours later I began to wake up from the anesthesia and I went into a panic because I couldn't breathe. I had cotton in both nostrils and my mouth was wired shut. The surgeon and two male nurses were holding me down as I came out of anesthesia. They knew it would be instinctual for me to want to open my mouth once I realized my nostrils were plugged with cotton rolls and no air was entering. That was exactly the case. I went into full Defcon panic and then the surgeon proceeded to calm me down and get me to focus on breathing through the side of mouth. Once I was somewhat calm, he explained that prior to the surgery he discovered my nose had also been broken and he needed to reset it during the surgery. In the end, I had a broken nose, broken jaw, two broken front teeth, bruised ribs, two black eyes and a big bump on my head. Chivalry was not dead, but it sure was beat up!

Due to the extent of my injuries, the incident was now considered a felony crime and the surgeon was required by law to call the police. That afternoon as I was recovering, two detectives arrived to investigate. It turned out that the responding officers failed to follow procedures, and this didn't sit well with the detective, so she filed a grievance with the department on my behalf. The responding police officers failed to take down the information of all parties involved and fill out a proper field report. This hampered their efforts in finding the assailants after my injuries elevated the assault to a felony. In the end, I was unable to work for 10 weeks. I was on a liquid diet for six of those weeks, accumulated a mountain of medical bills, and lost a lot of weight!

Whenever I tell this story, I usually get asked if I'd do it again. My answer is yes! But next time I won't turn away. I get comments such as "don't get involved," "no good deed goes unpunished," and so forth. But honestly, these guys were not up to any good with that girl and I probably saved her from them doing worse to her and I'm good with that. I have nieces and I would hope that if any of my nieces were ever in that situation, someone like me would step in.

5

Being Enough

'm not good enough, but I am! I've often said these words
to myself throughout my life, and I've often wondered if
I was enough, or why I wasn't enough? I recall the crush I
had when I was a teenager and the rejection of that person
not feeling the same toward me, and how it left me thinking
these words.

When I was young, I tried out for little league teams
for baseball and basketball (football looked too dangerous
for me, so I didn't even try going out for that!). I didn't
have good hand-eye coordination, and honestly, I really
didn't like sports that much, but I still went and tried out
for the teams just so I could hang out with my friends. I
always made the teams, but I figured it was just because the
coach was nice, or maybe that he saw something in me that
I could contribute to the game. Well, it turned out I did! I
contributed comic relief and comradery. I would use baseball bats as guitars and make up songs during practice to
make my teammates laugh and encourage them along the
way. I was that guy who always said, "That's okay, guys, we
will get them next time!" Yet, I usually didn't play. But the
times I did play I would be out in left or right field dancing

around, lost in my own world, and when the coach caught me and yelled out to me, I would get serious and concentrate on the next batter and pray very hard that he didn't hit the ball my way.

I wasn't good at sports, and I knew that; and yes, I did worry I wasn't enough. I had older brothers that excelled at sports, and because I already knew I was gay at that young age, I also believed that made me less of a person, and that I had to push myself harder just to be accepted.

At the end of those seasons, I was usually awarded the best sportsmanship award! Back then it was the award to just make you feel good and show that you were part of something. Looking back, it was my Oscar award for best performance!

Let me tell you about a recent incident with my photography that relates to this subject. I'm a street photographer and I usually photograph everyday life on the streets or capture moments of life as they occur. One day I decided to start working with people in a more controlled setting, a studio setting. I had never worked with models before, so this was a new thing to me. I wasn't too familiar with lighting either, but I was interested in creating a particular image, so I was going to try. I began to search for models, and I came across this one guy who I thought was just stunning. I chatted with him for a bit, and he agreed to be my model. I couldn't believe I had found someone who agreed to collaborate with me, especially since I wasn't a professional and it was going to be my first time working with lighting in a studio setting. Jake was his name. He had a beautiful face—stunning eyes, full lips—very handsome. The shoot was going to be in the nude and, at first, he was shy. We both agreed that his private parts would not show up in the final images. I wasn't going for pornography; this was an artistic photo shoot.

I had hesitated for years to explore this side of my photography skills because I believed I didn't have what it took. I didn't believe my work was good enough (even though I believe art is subjective to the viewer's interpretation). I always told myself that I wanted to reach a point with my photography that I would feel good enough for my images to hang on my own walls at home. I achieved this, but again, I felt I wasn't a good enough photographer to share my images with everyone else. After sharing my images of Jake on social media, I began to receive so many wonderful accolades and words of encouragement. I'm finally coming around to the feeling that I am good enough!

Another time when this lesson presented itself to me was not too long into my tenure of working with Neil Diamond. He had called a meeting with his department heads and tour management. It was my first meeting with everyone since joining the ranks. We were discussing various things regarding the upcoming tour. Throughout the meeting I was silent and didn't speak up. Then Neil asked for my input. I was stunned. Here I was having a meeting with Neil Diamond and all his key personnel that ran his tours. And although I was now part of that prestigious group of professionals, I was the new guy and the youngest

Jake (Los Angeles, 2021)

of them all, not to mention I was still questioning if I belonged there among these veteran professionals.

After a brief pause, I replied with, "Me? You want my opinion?" I could feel the eyes of everyone around the table fixated on me as they waited with anticipation for what the new guy was going to say. Neil then replied simply with, "Yes, I'm asking for your opinion. You're in your position because I feel you have something to offer, otherwise I wouldn't have put you there." He put his confidence in my abilities, and I realized that it was time that I needed to believe in those abilities and offer up my opinion with that same confidence. I did so and he liked what I had to say and discussed it further with the group. His confidence, trust, and respect are things I've always valued about him. It's what drove me to continue working with him for 10 years and strive to do the best I could with everything I was responsible for.

As I grew into my position (and eventually moved up into the position of road manager), I brought fresh ideas into the role. Although many times I would get serious push back from various members of the tour, Neil was always there to encourage me. He was bored with the old way of doing things and wanted new and fresh ideas on how things could be done.

I came to learn that believing in yourself is not just limited to believing in your ability to contribute but also to believing that you can make change in your own life. There was this one afternoon when I received a call from Neil Diamond's manager, Salvatore (Sal) Bonafede, a man that was well known and respected in the industry. And although I was just the newly appointed assistant road manager, I received a call from Sal inviting me to lunch. I was startled and surprised that I was being invited to lunch by this industry powerhouse. I remember questioning myself: Why was he inviting me to lunch? Was I getting fired already? I later found out that he just wanted to check in with me and see how I was doing in my new position. This led to somewhat of a routine where Sal would invite me to lunch to just chat and check in.

One time he called to set up another lunch appointment but only because he wanted to show me his new car. I still remember being amazed at the technology his car had. There was a slot for his flip phone to go into that would then download all his contacts so he could call anyone he wanted simply by scrolling to that person's name. After cruising around Beverly Hills, we then went to lunch at a restaurant where they held a table for him during the lunch hour. I was witnessing what the industry and the position he held in the industry could provide. Don't get me wrong, Sal wasn't showing off. He was just genuinely sharing and wanting me to see what the future could hold for me. He later gave me the advice that I shouldn't stay too long on the road; he believed I had what it would take to become a personal manager or more. He wanted to help me reach that potential and even went as far as inviting me to begin coming into his office to learn more about personal management. Unfortunately, weeks later, Sal unexpectedly passed away, and all those plans disappeared. The week Sal passed away we had scheduled to meet up for lunch but had postponed for the next week that would never come.

Sal never made me feel like I was anything less than the next guy and encouraged me to believe in myself and my abilities. He would remind me why I was in the position I was in and would always challenge me to continually raise the bar of my performance simply because I could and because of the importance of always striving for better.

Throughout my life I've operated like this: always striving for better. I come from a middle-class family upbringing of immigrant parents who worked hard to give me and my siblings an opportunity at a better life. They didn't hand it to us (believe me when I say this). My father made sure we earned it and recognized the difference between being handed it and earning it—thanks Dad. I grew up listening to a lot of the artists I've worked with, and I never thought I would find myself working with them, let alone traveling with them all over the world. I didn't set out to achieve this. I just made sure of one thing along the way: to do the best job I could do and that I was proud of. My dad used to tell me, "Remember, how well you do a job is your signature and the value of your signature is a reflection of who you are." And boy did my dad have an amazing signature, I always admired how he signed his name, but I now see how he was proud of the work he put out and why he was so well respected in the produce distribution industry.

MIND OVER MATTER . . .

. . . it only matters if you mind. Believing in yourself is a hard concept for many of us, but it's what counts when the challenges pile up. I'm still working on not letting what others think be the driving force of how I live my life.

Paddyism

"Whether you think you can or you can't, you're right."

Neil Diamond (Scotland 2008)

6

Was It Really the Butter?

*Y*ou ever go out to eat breakfast and once your food arrives you reach for your warm toast before it goes cold and then reach for the butter only to find it cold and hard? Then when you attempt to spread the said cold butter on your toast you are left with shreds of what once resembled toast?

Well . . .

It was around 5:00 a.m. and my phone rang in my hotel room—it was tour security calling to tell me the artist wanted to see me immediately in the hospitality suite! I was the assistant road manager at the time and in charge of advancing the hotel needs for the group. I was told the road manager was already enroute. I quickly threw some clothes on, splashed water on my face, did a quick chug of mouthwash and headed out the door to the suite. All the time I was thinking to myself, *What's going on? Why the early morning call? What's happened? Wow, is this what's it's going to be like being in tour management?*

I arrived to find the artist sitting at the breakfast table and he asked me to take a seat while we waited for the road manager to arrive (wouldn't you know it, my room

41

was closer, so I arrived before him). I noticed a hotel staff member standing there and asked him to leave, but the artist informed me he had asked him to stay . . . yikes!

The road manager finally arrived; then the artist proceeded to inform us that he woke up and came into the hospitality suite to have his breakfast and proceeded to prepare his toast to find out that the butter was cold and hard, and he couldn't spread it on his toast without it tearing apart the bread. He was upset and he let us have it. It was my first time being called on the line and all because the butter was cold . . . although it was more than that, but it was the straw that broke the camel's back, as the saying goes.

To be honest, I too dislike cold butter, but in that moment even more! Now every time I go to a restaurant or dinner event and cold butter is served, I chuckle and remember that moment with nothing but love.

There was more there than just cold butter, but that was the last thing that set it all off. Just like my back locking up on me, it wasn't the action of reaching for the paper that caused it, it was the slow build of stress over time that finally came calling when I took that action. It helps to take pause and search for the true root of our feelings to give us clarity on how to handle them. It's not easy to remember to do so, but with practice we can begin to achieve a greater percentage of time when we do.

7

Ordinary Things in Extraordinary Ways

hile we were waiting at the Chicago O'Hare International Airport, the artist I was with decided to take a walk around the terminal and, as usual, I accompanied her. We strolled for a bit and about 15 minutes into our walk, I noticed people recognizing her. They would take a second look, some would point and smile, but everyone gave her space. I was walking with her hand in my arm as we strolled and chatted about various things, and on occasion (more than not) we were laughing. It then hit me, I was at a major airport in the country, walking hand to arm and laughing with an iconic artist. I hadn't realized this because it was just the ordinary thing I do in my life and job. But right then I recognized how damn lucky I was and probably the envy of all those walking past us.

We came upon a kiosk, and she made a pit stop to check out its beautiful scarfs. She is a very playful, full-of-life person, so she was trying various scarfs on and asking my opinion if it looked good or not and at times throwing some on me as well to get a better look at them, or probably to make me blush (the latter surely happened). The attendant recognized her but didn't make it obvious until the end and was gracious about it. The artist selected a few scarfs she liked and was about to reach into to her purse to pay for them, when I asked her to please let me buy them for her and, in true spirit to her playful personality, she accepted and then turned to the attendant and informed her that her sugar daddy was going to pay for them. Again, I blushed, and we all laughed. The attendant thanked us and told the artist that she had made her day and that she was a big fan. We thanked her and began to make our way back to the airport lounge and all the time heads were turning, catching a glimpse of this iconic artist simply walking around the airport to stretch her legs.

Once we arrived back to the lounge, her husband, who always traveled with their dog named Trixie, quickly came up to me and informed me the doggie had to go do some "business." She was his support dog (way before support dogs became what they are now).

The thing with Trixie was that she didn't like to take care of business just anywhere, she needed real grass to do so—oh boy. We were in the middle of an airport; that was going to be a problem, because for us to go all the way outside to the front of the airport was not a viable option and who knew if we would even have found grass!

I took a chance and went up to the lounge staff to inquire if they had any suggestions. Of course, they were aware of who the artist was, and they were all very eager to help. Keep in mind this all took place in a time when airports didn't have indoor potty rooms like many do today. The staff made some calls and in minutes a ramp supervisor showed up, introduced himself, and escorted the husband, Trixie, and I to a car plane-side and then proceeded to drive us to a portion of the taxi runway area that was grassed so that Missy could do her business. I was blown away by this and so was the husband. He couldn't believe they did that! We laughed and talked about it for months afterward.

Again, my job is making things happen and seem ordinary, but in reality, they are extraordinary. Nothing to see here folks, just gonna take a car ride to the tarmac to take the dog out to do its business on the grass.

8

The Rumor Mill Tells Lies

This upcoming artist enjoys a good joke and playing prank jokes on others as well.

One time his manager and tour promoter went to dinner, but the rumor mill went into overdrive to spread the word that they had gone to a Lakers' basketball game that was taking place in the same arena the artist was going to perform in the following day! The rumor got to the artist, and he was a bit bothered that they had not extended an invitation to him or anyone else on tour.

This was when my phone rang, and I was sucked into becoming an accomplice in what was going to be an epic prank. The artist called me and asked me if I had access to their respective rooms. Me being the road manager and in charge of securing the hotels—of course I had that authorization and direct line of communication with the necessary hotel staff to obtain a key to each of their rooms. I was then instructed to be on standby and ready to enter their rooms within an hour.

Within 30 minutes I entered the first room along with the artist and a handful of staff and musicians to begin a transformation. First up was the manager's room. Among other things, we put Vaseline on the phone receiver, powdered sugar between the bed sheets, saran wrap on the toilet seat, and an alarm clock taped under the bed to go off at 3:00 a.m.! After that, we made our way over to the promoter's room and did the same thing. All these jokes were set up to be discovered as they utilized the rigged item.

We then retreated to our respective rooms. Everyone was looking forward to the next morning when the fury would be raised during breakfast. I, however, was in for a long night because I knew that my phone was going to be the one that would ring after the first prank was discovered, since any smart person would figure I had access to their rooms. I braced myself for the fury that would be unleashed on me. I had a great relationship with both of them so I knew whatever came my way wasn't personal, but I would have to work to correct things.

At around 11:00 p.m., after they returned to the hotel from dinner (not a Lakers' game), the first call came in. It was the promoter. At first, I heard laughter, then the question, "How did the artist get into my room?" He knew I was involved but also automatically knew the artist was behind all this. I tried to play dumb but that only lasted a few minutes before I broke out laughing after he told me how he discovered the first one . . . the toilet seat one . . . it was funny. At that moment my cell phone rang; it was the manager. I told the promoter who was calling, and his response was, "Oh no, did they do his room too?" I quickly answered my cell and all I heard was, "Come to my room immediately!"

I hung up both phones and immediately went to the manager's room.

When the manager answered his hotel door, he had a towel in his hand and was wiping Vaseline off his ear. Yup the phone prank was the one he'd discovered first; that's why he called my cell; he had already used his landline! He said, "Get in here," then preceded to rage on about why this had been done and why I had let them. He knew it was the artist who was the mastermind behind it all and he told me that I had better tell him what else was pranked. I of course had pledged to the artist that I wouldn't cave in, and I didn't. I was able to convince both the manager and the promoter that I only got them the keys and did not participate so I wasn't aware of the pranks they had set. He and I walked around the room in search of anything that looked suspicious. We found a few, but I didn't give in. The next morning, he called my room to tell me what other pranks he'd uncovered and made it clear he was not going to be responsible for any fees from the hotel if there were any damages. I assured him that he wouldn't. By the way, the artist had already told me to make sure any fees were put to his account, and he would pay them.

The next morning, I informed my hotel contact of the shenanigans and made sure to let them know the tour would pay for any damages. There were no damages, and they loved that the artist himself was the mastermind. They got a big laugh out of it.

At times the road can get long in the tooth and things like this help refocus on the fun of being on tour and life in general. Never believe rumors! And never act out because of them, especially if you are going to go to these lengths to get back at someone—egg on your face looks embarrassing. Yeah, it was later found out that everyone was misled with the rumor, but nobody took it hard, and we all had good laughs afterward and even played more practical jokes on each other down the road.

Paddyism

"Never lose the child within you;
it helps make life fun!"

9

Planning for the Unexpected

One of Paddy's sayings was that one should always be aware of their space and always have an escape plan. This is a story of that exact advice coming in very handy in the literal sense.

This artist I was working with was doing some shows in Las Vegas and there was a VIP meet and greet arranged for about 50–75 friends and industry people in a small meeting room of the casino convention center where he was performing.

The plan was simple: we would have all the people in the room mingling and then bring the artist in to say hi and take a few pictures.

I always make it a point to familiarize myself with the space I'm taking an artist into before I do so. Even though we had security and it would be very easy for me to leave that up to them, I always felt more comfortable reviewing things myself. When we did walk him into the room, it only took a few minutes before he was surrounded, and the situation quickly became a bit uncomfortable for him and me. The guests all wanted to say hi and take pictures with him all at once, even though we had made announcements about not rushing him.

The artist then looked over to me and whispered in my ear, "Get me out of here, now! I need a break!" I immediately motioned to security to get us out but unfortunately the path to the front entrance of the room was blocked and not easily passable. I quickly eyed one of the cocktail servers and remembered they had a back-of-the-house area where they were entering and exiting from. I quickly grabbed the server and asked him to walk us to the area and had security make a path to where the server was going. I then grabbed the artist and bolted in that direction. We were able to give him his private space to regroup and breathe before going back out and finishing his meet and greet.

The artist was very appreciative of my quick thinking and knowledge of the space. Things don't always go the way I expect them to or plan for, but the important thing is that I'm open to change. And, by planning, I give myself the ability to make changes to my plans versus trying to devise a plan on the fly. As with life, sometimes it helps to readjust how I look at things to get a better understanding of the situation.

POSTPONING A CONCERT

One time toward the end of a tour (after we finished a show in Tampa, Florida), the artist flew home on a private jet while the band and crew remained in Tampa for a few days off before flying to Houston for the next show.

The date that we flew to Houston would turn out to be one very long day for our travel agent Betty and myself. Upon arriving at the Houston airport, I turned on my cell phone to find it blowing up with messages from the artist's manager. I quickly reached out to him, and he informed me that the artist was sick and there were strong possibilities the last three remaining shows would need to be postponed. This delicate conversation was taking place as I was navigating my way through the airport to the baggage claim area along with 45 band and crew members in tow. As we waited for the luggage to come down the conveyor belt, I gathered the touring management staff together off to the side and informed them of the situation and began to formulate a plan. I was expecting one more call to confirm the decision before any plan could be executed.

While the staff focused on getting everyone's bags and getting the busses loaded to head over to a hotel, my first call was to my travel agent. I needed her to investigate the availability of flights to get everyone home the next day.

Once we boarded the bus and departed the airport, I received the call that solidified the decision to postpone the dates. I then informed the manager that my suggestion would be to get everyone home the next day so that we could reduce the economic impact the tour would be taking on. He agreed and gave me the green light to do what I needed to do.

I informed the staff to get the word out to everyone that once we arrived at the hotel, everyone was to meet in the hotel lobby for a mandatory meeting. There I informed everyone of what was developing and asked them to be on the lookout for their flight information to be delivered to their rooms before 5:00 a.m. Everyone was going home for the next week and a half while we rescheduled the dates and the artist recovered from his illness.

The travel agent and I worked through the evening into the late hours booking flights for everyone the next day. All this last-minute booking of flights was not an easy task and clearly took several hours. And, as Murphy's Law would have it, it was the day before our travel agent was scheduled to fly out of town to start her vacation!

Once we got everyone booked, it was time to begin moving things around: hotels, trucks, equipment, and so on. At this point I decided to move over to Dallas, Texas, and work out of the hotel we were supposed to check into since I couldn't get a full cancelation on the rooms. I, along with our production coordinator, Amber, hunkered down for the next week moving things around.

Thinking quickly on my feet, staying focused, and remaining calm are strong skills I have developed over the years. This came to serve me well during this situation. Making decisions that affect others can be difficult at times, and it can cause me to pause and second-guess myself, which could lead to being indecisive and losing the confidence of those who depend on me to lead. I always work to gather information from those around me who I trust and who hold more expertise in the area that I'm having to decide on before I move forward. I don't pretend to know it all.

This is where believing in myself is very important. For others to have confidence in me and follow me, I must be confident in my decisions. This doesn't mean I have to be 100 percent right; it just means I need to evaluate all the factors at hand, make the best-informed decision, and be confident in that.

Paddyism

"Establish your perimeter, your zone of influence, and always scope out your exit route."

10

Follow the Thread

R ent a yacht for the day . . . yeah, that's what Neil
Diamond asked me to do at 8:00 p.m. one evening after
we arrived in Tampa, Florida.

It all started with him calling me into his room to open
the windows in his suite. Many hotels in those days would
bolt the windows due to jumpers, and sometimes we would
get special permission to open them, after signing a release
form, of course. This time around, I had forgotten to unlock
them prior to him entering his suite so he called me and
asked me to do so.

While I was unlocking the windows, we both noticed
the amazing yachts on the marina below. We started com-
paring which ones each of us liked and discussing why. Then
out of nowhere, he said, "Hey, Artie, why don't you look into
renting one for tomorrow for us to cruise around the bay for
the day?" I was like, "Are you serious?" Of course, he was
serious. He wanted me to secure one big enough to fit the
entire touring entourage (crew, band, staff, and, of course,
him!) along with food and drinks so it could be a day off
relaxing on the water. Cast off time was to be 1:00 p.m.!

Now, it was 8:30 p.m. by the time I finished unbolting the windows and before I could begin trying to contact any of the yacht owners, that is, if I could at all. This is when I went into "follow the thread" mode and started by contacting the manager on duty at the front desk and enlisting his help. "Follow the thread" is a phrase/methodology a former boss taught me. It refers to finding something that is connected to the answer I seek (the tip of the thread) and following its connection down the line (thread) until I find the answer. This has served me well throughout my entire career.

In this case, I decided to seek the "tip of the thread" by speaking to the hotel. I figured that surely, they had some contact with some of these yacht owners. After speaking to them, I took a walk around the marina and began to write down names and registration numbers of the yachts I thought would be big enough for us to use so I could go to the marina office and do my best to get their contact information.

I would later discover that Neil's idea was not original to the location. It seemed that idea pops into many guys' heads when visiting the hotel and casting eyes on these beautiful water oases. Unfortunately, it seemed this idea often popped into the heads of guys at the bars surrounding the marina, and let's just say they had already had a few ounces of the liquid bravado and were trying hard to impress the fair maiden they were each with. This of course led to many late calls to owners about their desires, only for the owners to then be left stranded on the dock and never taking voyage.

Yes, big talkers with small wallets! So, as I reached out to owners, I was immediately met with the "oh, here comes another one" attitude, which I understood.

I had to get creative and to be willing to reveal my identity to these owners so that they would take me seriously. Revealing my identity (I mean telling them I was the road manager for Neil Diamond) was something I didn't go around spreading loosely, for security purposes. After informing them of my hotel location and desire, there would be a brief rolling of the eyes (yeah, I could hear it in their voices). I would then inform them of who I was and who I represented and instructed them to feel free to call the hotel main line and ask for the manager on duty and ask to be connected to me and he would verify that I was who I said I was and would connect them to my room. The first call I received started with, "Oh shit, you are for real!" and then a burst of laughter from both of us. I continued this routine until I had contacted the 3 top yachts I had selected while following the thread and walking the marina and writing down their names and registration numbers. This continued for a while as it would take some time for the owners to look into things to ensure they could provide the service I was asking for.

By 12:00 a.m. I finally had my list of options ready to present to Neil for final selection. I rang his room, and he invited me over to present everything and make a decision. After a brief discussion, we had a winner! I ran to my room to make the call and lock it in as it was already creeping close to 1:00 a.m. and we still had to notify the touring entourage of the amazing excursion we had just planned for a 1:00 p.m. launch! (Yeah, let's just say I didn't get much sleep since I had to be up very early to work on all the preparations and coordinate who was joining us and so forth.)

The time came for the main voyage (cue the Gilligan's Island theme song) and we were off on our three-hour cruise, but I actually think it was more like four hours. We spent the time cruising the bay, eating some great food, and drinking to our hearts' content. It was a great bonding moment, with lots of laughs, views, and relaxation.

This wasn't the only time I had to organize this. We repeated this in London as well and that was just as magical. Yes, I worked my butt off to make it happen and even on the cruise I still had to play partial host working with the yacht's crew while everyone else lounged, but it was worth it to see everyone's faces filled with relaxation and joy. This is just one of the many perks in this line of work and I wouldn't trade it for anything.

Neil Diamond on Yacht
(River Thames, London 2008)

Art @ Yacht (Tampa 2005)

11

It's the Journey, Not the Destination

On one occasion we were in the process of moving the touring party from London to Birmingham (which was just a three-hour drive via the charter bus I had arranged). The idea was that we were going to board the bus and stop along the way at a roadside tavern, something the bus driver would arrange. Across the United Kingdom there are taverns and inns along the road that make great places to stop and have a meal and a pint or two, providing quite a wonderful experience while traveling in the United Kingdom.

Two days before we were supposed to travel, the artist pulled me aside and asked me to investigate the possibility of traveling by train instead of bus so that we could make the trip more enjoyable and scenic. I immediately knew this was going to be a challenge—moving 20 plus people on a public train, including a highly popular artist who was on tour performing to sold-out audiences in arena and soccer stadiums. Well, the good thing was that we had a security team traveling with us who would do their best to secure him during our move. I reached out to our travel agent Tina to inquire about securing tickets for everyone and to give me the lowdown on what it's like traveling on this train and route. It wasn't going to be easy; it was all coach seating and first come, first serve regarding seats! Oh boy! Looked like somebody wasn't going to have a seat if the train was full!

I had the travel agent purchase all the tickets. I would just go over to the train station and pick them up the morning of our departure. Then came the next challenge the artist presented me with; he wanted to make sure there was food of some kind available for our group. Well, this train did not have a café cart as some trains have. Great! Now I needed to figure out something for our group. After discussing this with the staff (security, tour manager, assistants) we came up with the idea of just having our catering staff prepare various sandwiches, chips, and drinks for us to carry and hand out.

I set out early in the morning to get to the station to collect the tickets and check it out and map out our route from the point of drop off to the actual track where we would board the train. I also wanted to scope out the surroundings and the crowds. Yup, just as I suspected, it was a very busy day and was only going to get busier as it continued. Oh well, we were committed already, and it had to happen.

Security and I had it all mapped out and had various contingent plans for various scenarios. Now it was time to move the group. The idea was to keep it low key and just move like two separate groups to not draw too much attention. To my surprise the tour manager handed out bright red caps to everyone so that we could keep an eye on each other and not lose anyone! Well, there went the idea of keeping it low key. Nothing like a bunch of Americans wearing red baseball caps making their way through a crowded train station to keep it chill and not attract attention. Despite my protests of this "great idea," some members of the group participated in the cap wearing, while others saw my point and refused. Well, against those odds, we made it on the train without a hitch, other than some folks having to stand because of lack of seats. To lighten the mood, I handed out sandwiches like a ballpark hot dog vendor.

About an hour and half into the journey, our train came to a slow crawl, moving ever so slowly. The conductor came on the PA and informed us that he was slowing down due to traffic on the tracks up ahead. Okay this was common, no big deal. Well, we continued moving slower and slower and then boom! A complete stop. I thought to myself, *now what?!* We sat there for a bit expecting for the conductor to announce something, but we only heard the constant chatter from all the passengers on the train. We waited for about 10 minutes then the conductor finally announced that we would have to stay put while they cleared the traffic up ahead and that it could be an hour before we might continue our journey. Oh boy, this was not good. Keep in mind that this was summer in the United Kingdom and with the train turned off, the air conditioner didn't work. Everyone began to open windows to get some air circulation going. I went over to check on the artist to ensure he was doing okay, which he was, but then he looked over to me and asked me to see what I could find out about moving the group along. The doors didn't work, and I couldn't get between cars, so I was left to trying to look out for the conductor or any train staff member to inquire about us getting off. At this point I finally realized I was going to have to go out and locate my answers—this meant me escaping out a small window. With the help of two security staff members, I was lifted in horizontal position and passed through the window feet first so that I landed safely and could walk to the front of the train and talk with the conductor.

As I landed on my feet, I looked toward the front of the train and noticed we were just yards away from a small train station platform where I saw a train staff member. I made my way over to him. As he saw me, he panicked and asked me how I got out, proclaiming that I shouldn't be off the train. I informed him of my escape procedure and then proceeded to make my inquiries. He informed me that another train farther ahead on the tracks had broken down and that's why our train was stopped. I pointed out how close we were to the platform and asked why we didn't just move the train a bit so that we could exit. He said they couldn't do that, yet he didn't give a reason for it. At this point it was time for me to drop the artist's name and the fact that he was on the train along with members of his tour. He was surprised to hear this and said he would go talk to the conductor about this. At this time one of the security staff members (Jason) walked up; he had exited out the window as I had. After looking around, we both saw the station was nothing more than a building with no services to offer waiting passengers, so I had him walk up the road and try to locate a place we could take refuge in while I contacted the charter bus to make its way to us to pick us up and get us to our destination.

I returned to the train and informed the rest of the staff what was happening and made sure nobody else got off the train because we didn't want to upset the conductor. Just then I saw the train staff member making his way back toward where I was. He informed me that the conductor would move the train to the platform for folks to get off. Great! I made my way back to the platform so that I was off the tracks and the train could safely move. This took a few minutes. Then my phone rings; it was Jason. He informed me he had located a tavern called The Swan Inn a few blocks away and it served food and beer and only had two patrons in it. I asked him to call the bus driver and give him the address so he could make his way to us. The train began to move slowly and made its way to the platform. The doors opened, and everyone flooded out. I met up with the director of security and the artist and gave them the details of where the tavern was located and that the bus driver had been called and was making his way to the inn to take us to our destination. He agreed with everything, and we gathered everyone and instructed them to follow the leader to the tavern for food and drink! What a sight it was to see everyone walking along the sidewalk en route to a tavern. We arrived at the tavern, and everyone was in good spirits despite all that had happened; but then again, it was out of our control, and we only controlled our reactions to it.

The look on the proprietor's face when he saw all of us walking in was a sight of confusion and surprise. This small-town roadside tavern suddenly was filled with all these Americans and one rock star!

This day turned out to be a very long day for me. As the road manager, I was tasked with handling all the logistics for the tour, moving everyone safely from one destination to another. On this day, I was challenged. When I look back on this story, I see some of my growth as a person from my days working at my parents' grocery store. From a young age I've had this thing for organization and my mother recognized this while I was working alongside her at our grocery store. She encouraged me to keep using my organizational skills and began to hand me more responsibilities at the store. I was even given the responsibility at the age of 17 to open and close the grocery store and work with the vendors placing orders. Because of this experience and my planning and organizational skills, on this day of train trouble I was able to view the big picture of the situation and make the necessary adjustments calmly and confidently to get us back on track (no pun intended) and get us to our destination. I've often said to others that detail planning allows me to be open to the unexpected and deal with it with confidence. If I have a plan, then I can review and adjust to reroute myself and get back on track; but if I don't have a plan, then I will find myself lost, confused, and panic stricken trying to figure things out.

Funnily enough, the bus driver later told me that The Swan Inn was the same tavern we were going to stop at if we had taken the bus in the first place. Six hours later we made it to our hotel in Birmingham, United Kingdom, three hours longer than it would have taken us if we had just taken the bus. But, then again, it's the journey not the destination that is important. This journey presented us with a great bonding moment and one I remember fondly.

12

IRAQ-2009

*I*n 2009 I was fortunate to be able to go with an artist to Iraq as part of a USO (United Service Organization) performance tour for our country's military troops.

This trip has been the highlight of my career for so many reasons: first and foremost because I was part of a team bringing entertainment to our troops during a war in another country. I was able to witness firsthand what our troops go through and get a small sense of the danger they face. Now, please understand, I say a small sense because it's nothing compared to what the troops face daily. We were well cared for and protected, and I never felt unsafe. I believe with all my heart that our military is amazing, and I was very happy to know they had our backs.

Preparing for the trip was a big task, mentally and logistically. On the mental side we had to wrap our brains around the fact that we were headed to a war zone. I also had to write a will and leave it with family just in case . . . Yeah, that shook up my family a bit.

The logistics were challenging because we were limited on what we could take, yet I needed to make sure the artist had everything he and his band needed to put on a performance to the artist's standards. I couldn't ship any-thing via our regular shipper. We had to carry everything with us on the flight we were taking, so it all had to be checked baggage. It took a few calls to the airline to be able to secure space for all the musical equipment we needed to take with us, but I got it done. The USO organizers were surprised with how much gear and luggage I was able to get checked in and allowed by the airline.

We flew commercial from Los Angeles to Frankfurt, Germany, then on to Kuwait. Once in Kuwait, we spent the night at a hotel that was a fortress. It was a small compound of two hotels and restaurants that was heavily guarded by military. The next day we were driven in a heavily guarded convoy of suburban and military vehicles that stuck close together and drove fast and never stopped until we reached the military base that was two hours away and where we would then board a military aircraft to take us to Baghdad. I recall the lieutenant who was riding in our vehicle, a short woman with lots of spunk. She leaned over to the driver, who happened to be a local, and with a firm direct tone instructed him to stay close to the vehicle in front and NEVER under any circumstance stop. US military convoys were under ongoing threat. It was an intense ride to say the least.

Once we arrived in Baghdad at Camp Victory, we were taken to our hotel. It turned out to be Saddam Hussein's hunting lodge that was converted into a hotel for visit-ing guests and transitioning military officers. This place was huge!

We were issued helmets and Kevlar vests that we had to wear anytime we were outside of a building. We were escorted everywhere by a squad of soldiers who were heavily armed as well. We were there for 10 days. We flew on C-17 aircrafts, Chinooks, Blackhawk helicopters, and rode in Humvees and a bulletproof suburban. It was a wild ride every time we were transported to various locations.

During our downtime we hit golf balls off the back porch into a huge pond, we toured the compound, and some of the guys even played basketball with some of the soldiers. We never knew exactly where we were going; that was information that they kept secret for security reasons. We would just be told what time we needed to be ready to board the vehicles for our move. The gear was moved prior to our move so it would already be there once we arrived. Sometimes the artist and his band would perform for a big crowd and sometimes a small one at a FBO (fixed-base operator). There was always time for meeting the troops either before or afterward and that was a great treat to see. The faces of the men and women would light up just saying hi and meeting the artist and band and even the small crew we took with us. They were just happy to see people from their home country visiting them. And if one of us was from their home state or city, it was an even bigger treat for them.

One of the highlights was that we were there when President Obama was inaugurated as the 44th president. It was a great experience to be among our country's military as a new commander in chief was sworn in. Of all places to be to witness a new president take office, this was only second to being at the inauguration in Washington, D.C. I noticed how the troops showed tremendous respect for George W. Bush while he was still their commander-in-chief, but once Barrack Obama took the oath of office and became their new commander-in-chief, their tone toward the outgoing one was very evident.

At night we would sometimes hear gunfire out in the distance. For me it brought things back to reality and delivered a stark reminder that we were in a real war zone.

One evening while the artist was performing at a FBO for a small group, I was informed we were going to have to cut the performance short and move out and fly back to base camp. I informed the artist to cut his set short and get to the hits. Afterward we piled into the vehicles and drove to the location where the Chinook helicopters would be picking us up. As we arrived at the location, the lieutenant that oversaw our escort informed me that the helicopters that were assigned to pick us up were rerouted to an emergency mission and we were going to have to wait a bit longer. He apologized for the inconvenience, which in return I said, "No need to apologize. I'd rather that helicopter go on a mission for our troops than to come pick us up just to transport us to the base. We are no more important than our troops." He smiled and said, "Thank you."

We waited for a few hours and eventually some of us fell asleep waiting; except for our escorts of course; they were always alert and on duty. After a few hours the lieutenant then told me he had just received a message that the helicopters were 10 minutes away. We woke up everyone and prepared to leave the vehicles. Standing there half asleep, we were informed that once the signal was given, we would run to the helicopters and board quickly so that they could take off swiftly. They didn't want them sitting on the ground too long.

As we all stood outside of the vehicles awaiting the arrival of the helicopters, I couldn't see anything in the pitch-dark desert night. We were in total darkness for safety reasons. I could barely see my hand in front of me! The immediate space around us was filled with silence, yet in the distance I faintly heard the war. Then out of nowhere, I heard a loud thumping sound, the sound of two massive propellers. Then out of nowhere the lights of the aircraft came on and it landed right in front of us. They quickly switched to green lights, and we were given the signal to run, and run we did!

We boarded the aircraft quickly then, once we were all seated, the ramp lifted to close halfway and the gunner (yes, GUNNER!) who was at the end directly across from me gave me a thumbs up as we took off. He then lowered his night vision goggles and manned his machine gun. This was serious business, and yeah, at this time my heart was racing. I think it was part fear and part excitement. When they shot off flares I really freaked out, as did everyone else, but we were quickly reassured to stay calm and that it was just a precautionary tactic. I remember sitting at the tail end of the helicopter looking out into the darkness with faint lights scattered amongst it and hearing the loud thumping of the helicopter and thinking, *This is why I wrote my will, just in case!*

We made it back to camp, exhausted and a bit frazzled, but safe and sound. The next day I asked the lieutenant about the flares, and he informed me that they do that just in case a missile is shot at the aircraft. The flares are a deterrent for the heat-seeking missiles. Yeah, not extra comforting but still relieved we made it home.

Thank you to all our military that
sacrifices so much for our country.

Art in military helmet
and bullet vest (Iraq 2009)

U.S. Soldiers at concert (Iraq 2009)

Art in Saddam Hussein's chair in Baghdad (Iraq 2009)

U.S. Blackhawk over Baghdad (Iraq 2009)

13

Never Actually Quit

*T*his artist was young and relatively new to the business when he was quickly thrust into a high level of international popularity and onto the world's stage. I had already been in the business for over 10 years and been working with many A-list artists and was very familiar with the road and everything that came with it. I was called by his management representatives and asked if I would be interested in working with him on his first tour. At first, I hesitated simply because of his huge popularity and lack of experience in touring at the high level he was about to embark on. It looked like a recipe for someone's head to blow up and become a challenge, but I ended up agreeing and I jumped into the role of tour manager, teacher, and advisor for not only the artist but his band as well.

As the tour progressed, so did his popularity, and this is where his view on things began to change. Suddenly, he thought he was more knowledgeable than I was and began to challenge me and override some of my decisions.

I should clarify that the artist is ultimately the boss; everyone (and I mean everyone, including management, agent, tour manager, and so on) works for them. However, remember that in many cases I hire certain people for their level of expertise/knowledge in a specific area and I need to work to trust and listen to their guidance. They have been down the proverbial road many times and they are only advising where the potholes and bumps are along the road.

The final moment where I knew it was time to take myself out of the equation was when he became upset about something (I can't remember exactly what), and he came backstage and yelled at me with everyone around to witness. Many things led to this moment, and I wasn't going to allow anyone to treat me like that, so I shared with him my thoughts on the situation in the same manner. It stunned everyone, including him and myself. I had never behaved that way before, but I also wasn't going to allow someone who was newly minted into his fame dismiss my years of experience and speak to me as if I didn't matter.

After the blow up, I reached out to management and informed them of what had transpired and that a replacement for me was in order. They appreciated my call and agreed and would begin searching for my replacement immediately. They asked if I would/could remain on tour until they could secure someone, and I agreed. I knew I would have to go to the artist and make amends so that we could get through the week until a replacement was secured. I did so and he agreed to me sticking around until my replacement was secured and he thanked me for doing what he knew I didn't have to do.

After I had spoken to management, I reached out to my mentor, Patrick Stansfield, and discussed what had transpired, just wanting to get it off my chest. Patrick was always just a phone call away for comfort, advice, and a good old stern wake-up call. After I explained to him everything that had occurred, he reminded me of one of his road rules (Paddyisms). He reminded me that it's okay to threaten to quit, but to NOT ACTUALLY quit! In this case, I had already done so and there was no turning back, so he simply said, walk tall and leave with dignity and grace.

On my final day, we had an outdoor show. As we waited for showtime to arrive, everyone was either resting up or doing busy work. I walked out of the production office trailer and spotted the artist sitting in a golf cart away from everyone staring out into the horizon watching the sunset. The colors were amazing—reds, oranges, yellows—and the clouds added texture to the sky. It was a peaceful, beautiful view, so I walked over and sat next to him. He turned to me and commented on the amazing sunset as did I. We both realized what had happened was not right, but he understood where I was coming from and thanked me for that. I shared with him some of the knowledge my mentor had shared with me throughout my years. He was new to this whole fame and touring world, and he knew it. I guess he was just trying to show everyone he knew what he was doing to justify his existence in the role he was thrust into. His talents got him there, but his knowledge of the business still trailed far behind. I on the other hand had all this experience and was acting just like him, trying to prove I knew better and justifying my own existence in my role as well. He thanked me for my honesty and the advice I shared with him, and we hugged, and I left him alone to enjoy the rest of the sunset in peace.

We both didn't have to behave the way we did to get the respect we each thought we deserved. It's okay to not have all the answers and it's also okay to admit you are still learning. It's also good to remember that everyone must start somewhere and those farther along should be patient and understanding of the growth that others still need to go through.

Just because I was yelled at by the artist didn't mean I wasn't respected by others, nor did it make me less knowledgeable. I allowed my ego to get in the way of me fulfilling my job of tour manager, teacher, and advisor. And on his part, the artist didn't have to know everything or act like he did just because he was the artist. I guess we both allowed our egos dictate how we were supposed to be instead of us just being ourselves. I don't have to be X to get Y. What the X and Y represent is for you, the reader, to decide. I learned I didn't have to actually quit to make my point, nor did I have to have all the answers to lead.

Paddyism

"It is okay in difficult circumstances to threaten to quit a project based on moral or artistic or ethical reasons or for any reason really if you have to, to carry your point, but you must remember to never actually quit!"

14

Words with Friends the Boss

We missed our flight because of the game Words with Friends! k.d. lang and I were traveling from one city to another via commercial flight while on tour during the time that the game Words with Friends was all the rage. We were sitting across from our boarding gate, and because we got there early, as any good tour manager would always ensure, we decided to play a few rounds of the game.

We are both competitive. We got so into the game that we didn't hear the PA calls for us to board the flight—some good tour manager I was. After I handed her my phone for her turn at the game, I looked up and noticed the waiting area was empty. My stomach dropped. I noticed the gate agent walking over to us. As she approached us, she smiled and said, "Ms. Lang? Mr. Cisneros?" I looked around and it was just us two in the waiting area. I'm sure she recognized k.d., then again it probably wasn't hard for her to deduce our identities in an empty waiting area. I responded with, "Oops yeah, that's us." She proceeded to tell us she had been calling us on the PA alerting us to the plane boarding. We admitted we were just too focused on our game and didn't hear her nor did we realize the time lapse.

Oops we missed our flight. I looked over at k.d. and we both laughed and realized no sense crying over spilled milk. The agent informed us that she would rebook us on the next flight that was departing in one hour, so we just made our way over to the next gate and sat there attentively so we wouldn't miss this one.

k.d. taught me the importance of slowing down in life and being in the moment, and how to meditate using my malas while chanting two different mantras. I would travel with her from city to city on commercial flights and she would always see me working on my computer or phone every minute, only to continue and increase in intensity once we arrived at the venue. One day while on a flight, she playfully pulled my laptop screen down to turn it off. I reopened it and she closed it again. This repeated a few times, just like two kids in the backseat of their parents' minivan. I finally asked her to stop and explained that I needed to work, and she said, "No, you don't have to work; you want to work." She asked what was so important that I had to work on that minute. I informed her what it was (it was really something that could wait but I was trying to stay ahead of the workload). I usually had everything set in advance for our daily travels.

She asked me to not work and just be. She asked me to put my computer away and to just sit there and enjoy the flight and talk with her. So, I did and then she said, "I'd like you not to work when we travel. I want you to take life in and experience the journey." That was deep for me. I ended up asking her about her malas and meditation practice and before you knew it, I was meditating.

I began to lighten my load of things I carried when we flew and didn't turn on my computer. She gifted me for my birthday the latest Blackberry I had my eyes on and that made it so easy for me to answer emails and work more on the fly and be able to sit back and enjoy the journey.

Working with her taught me so much about experiencing the journey of life. I'll forever be grateful to her for introducing me to and teaching me meditation. I would grow to embrace it further and continue to expand my practice as years would come. It's been what has helped me keep it together all these years.

Thank you, k.d.

k.d. lang at rehearsals (San Diego 2007)

15

The Artist

I've walked many of the artists I've worked with on and off the stage. With many of them, I've noticed a transformation that happens while they are on stage. It's like they become this other person and when they come off the stage, I notice that it's not the same person I walked onto the stage. I've stared into the eyes of some, and I could see that this transformation had taken place. Because of this, they usually require a few minutes alone in their dressing rooms immediately after coming off stage to decompress and come back to themselves. It doesn't happen all the time, but when it does it's a very amazing thing to witness.

Many times, artists come off the stage feeling that the performance they just gave was horrible and they get concerned that the audience hated the performance or noticed this or that mistake. Some of the audience might catch this or that mistake, but honestly, I believe they are so excited to see the show and are just enjoying themselves that they really don't let it bother them. Perfection is something that many artists are always striving for, as the rest of us are with our own lives, searching for the perfect partner, home, job, life.

One thing I've learned from my career is that what I see or hear on the stage or screen isn't always the true reflection of real life. An artist isn't immune to feeling pain, anger, sadness, loneliness, disappointment, and many other discomforts like the rest of us. Sometimes they must face some of life's challenges in the public eye and that can be even more challenging.

I do my best at engaging the artist I work with like I would with everyone else. I am not afraid to say no or offer my thoughts on something even if it's probably not what I believe they want to hear. I respect their talents and expertise, but I too have my own talents and expertise and that is why they employ me. I like to consider myself a collaborator and not a yes-man, and collaborators sometimes have to agree to disagree.

Paddyism

"The artist spends an enormous amount of their life looking for the person that appears when the lights go on, on stage, and disappears when the lights go off. Some artists go their whole life trying to find that person who in fact only exists when the audience, the lights, the sound, are in show condition."

Artist on stage (Portugal 2010)

16

A Prop Too Big

*I*n 2009, this artist whom I was working with was doing her first US Tour. The promoter, who just happened to be one of the nicest people in the music industry, hired me to be the promoter representative on the road. My responsibility was to represent the promoter on the road and ensure the artist and her team were taken care of and that the shows went smoothly.

One of the first tasks I had was to fly to Montreal, Canada, and look into the redesigning of a large prop that had just been used for her arena/stadium tour overseas. It was too large to fit into the theatres we were going to be going into so it had to be scaled down and also made lighter so that it could be suspended from the ceiling. It was a big undertaking, and I had to go there to check in and gather details so that back at the office we could investigate each venue and ensure it would fit and safely be suspended from the ceiling.

As we landed in Las Vegas in preparation for the second show, I turned on my cell phone to reveal several texts and voicemails from the office. Something was up. Once I was in a place to speak freely (off the plane and in the terminal)

I called the office and was informed that one of the future venues had sent us wrong information and there was a strong probability that the prop would not fit in that venue. This prop was a vital part of the show and it wasn't like we could just not use it. I told him I was just making my way to the luggage claim area with the rest of the touring party. He then informed me the office had already purchased me a flight to Chicago so I could get there and assess the venue situation and rectify it. I quickly grabbed my bag then went up to the tour manager and production manager and informed them of the situation.

Once I made it to Chicago, I grabbed a rental car and headed straight to the venue. It turned out the venue was old and, yep, it wouldn't be able to sustain the weight of the prop from the ceiling, so I was now tasked with finding a venue that was available for the same date of the show so we wouldn't have to move the date. Fortunately for me, the office had already been working on talking to various venues around town and had put together a short list of venues that had that date open and had the capacity we needed.

After driving around from venue to venue and crossing them off the list for various reasons, I finally came to a small college arena. It was bigger than we needed but we would be able to hang the prop and fit the production in without any issues. The only other issue was all the extra seats that came with the venue. It was a much larger venue, and we didn't want the place to look empty. Ticket sales had been great for all the tour and in this city, we were almost at a sell out, so it was pitched to the artist's manager that it would provide an opportunity to sell more tickets and make the move look like the change was because of the sell out and we wanted to open it up to more fans. He agreed, and we locked it in.

We sold the additional tickets, the place was nicely filled, and the show was a hit! This was one of the most exciting tours I have done simply because I wasn't responsible for the entire tour, but I was a vital part in making sure the tour went off without a hitch.

17

Brace for Impact!

I love the smell of fresh baked bread; it's just so welcoming and comforting to the soul. I wouldn't expect that to be the smell I'd be welcomed with when boarding a tour bus— but if your bus driver is John Clarke, that is certainly what you will get every time after a show. This baker is also the man who saved our lives one evening after a show.

We were on the freeway making the transition onto a highway heading out of town. Huey Lewis and the band were in the front lounge hanging out, eating bread and revisiting the show they had just completed. I was in the jump seat (the seat next to the driver), which is my favorite place to be as we leave a city. It's my way of saying good-bye to another day and show.

On this particular late evening we were the lead bus with the crew bus following right behind us en route to our next destination. Sometime after the road transitions, our fearless driver John noticed a car begin to flip on the other side of the highway and although we had a good two-lane-width dirt median between the inbound and outbound lanes John had a distinct feeling there was potential for danger. He immediately got my attention and told me to warn everyone to brace for impact. I hadn't seen that the car had jumped the median and didn't realize it was heading toward us until he mentioned it. I immediately yelled to the band to brace for impact while I was doing the same. That's when I noticed the dust cloud the car created as it barreled toward us. A cloud of uncertain danger; I didn't know what type of vehicle was within that dust cloud, but I did know it wasn't a good thing.

John proceeded to maneuver the 45-foot bus from one lane to another and at the same time grabbed his radio microphone to inform our crew bus behind us of the impending danger. At that moment the car came into my view as it rolled multiple times, exiting the large cloud of dust and landing on its roof. It slid toward the front of our bus as John swerved, just missing the impact and safely bringing our bus to stop on the side of the road a few yards away from where the car came to a complete stop. Our crew bus was also able to avoid contact and stopped short of where the car came to rest.

After ensuring all our passengers were safe and unharmed, I turned to notice debris scattered all over the street including a shoe, this made me cringe as I feared what I was going to find outside. John and I rushed to the car to aid the driver and any potential passengers. We arrived to find a young college kid alive and trying to get out through the window. Other drivers from various cars were already onsite helping him escape the wreckage. I ran back to the bus to grab a blanket to cover him as we waited for the emergency vehicles to arrive. This kid was lucky; he wasn't seriously injured besides a few scratches. I then noticed the shoes I saw on the highway were from his gym bag as it was thrown out of the vehicle—that was a big relief to me.

After a brief talk with the emergency personnel, we were allowed to leave. When we all got back on the bus, we took a breath to take in what had just happened and what we had just avoided. Our amazing driver John had commanded this 45-foot long, 53,000-plus pound tour bus with amazing skill so that none of us were further injured, on board or in the already in turmoil vehicle as it flipped uncontrollably.

Huey then poured me a shot of whisky to bring my adrenaline down and we were off again on the road.

It's easy to forget that what we do has its dangers just like anything else in life. I've had friends and colleagues in actual bus crashes, hotel fires, plane crashes, stage accidents, and so on. Safety is of vital importance and taking all necessary precautions sometimes doesn't prevent all accidents. That's why I believe it's important to recognize when they are averted and those involved in preventing them.

My emergency response training from the hotel industry has always stuck with me, and my observation of the many situations I've witnessed has also had a lasting impression on me. This is why I jumped into action as I did when all this happened; it just comes second nature to me. I make it a point to continually learn and stay informed of all aspects of my industry, including lifesaving procedures.

18

Thoughts of Suicide

*I*n late December 2011, one of my childhood friends whom I was very close to passed away suddenly. He was the funny one in my small group of friends I grew up with and continued our friendship beyond our college years. His death was a shock to us all, although something tells me he knew of his early exit but chose not to tell anyone. His name was Jaime.

Jaime was always full of life and always making everyone around him laugh and encouraging them to enjoy life. He did just that; he enjoyed life to the fullest and at times he would comment to me that I was too serious and needed to let loose. I wasn't always too serious, but somewhere along my life's journey I guess I felt I needed to be more serious so that the world would take me seriously and I could hide in plain sight. Jaime knew I was gay. He was the only one of my close friends that knew my secret. He was massively loved by many people and had a great deal of friends and made friends everywhere he went. He was a gem.

I flew to my hometown to pay my respects at his funeral and mourn with my close friends. I stayed for the new year and then flew back to Los Angeles to focus on a touring project I had just accepted. I couldn't get Jaime out of my mind and simply couldn't comprehend why he died.

As I began working on organizing the tour, I began to have problems concentrating on every task. At times I would find myself drifting away in thought and then bursting out in tears as I thought of my friend. This continued for several weeks as I struggled to keep it all together. Then one day, it all fell apart on me. I was sitting at my desk reviewing emails and organizing my daily tasks when I began to feel my anxiety rise and this volcano of energy began to mount. I knew I needed to release this energy, so I decided to go for a run and get it out and get my daily exercise in as well. After my run I returned and, after a brief review of my emails, decided to lay down on the couch for a bit.

I woke up several hours later. I was shocked at how long I was asleep and quickly realized I had just wasted an entire day. I jumped to my desk to work and noticed the large number of extra emails and the number of missed calls and voicemails that had come in while I was asleep. At this moment I felt my body temperature beginning to rise, my skin felt prickly and on fire, I couldn't think straight, and I had trouble knowing what was happening. I then got a moment of clarity and figured it would be best to jump in the tub to cool off and regulate my body temperature. I rushed into the bathroom and turned the water on at full stream and didn't wait for the tub to fill before stripping off all my clothes and climbing into the tub and settling into the cool water and splashing it all over me in a frantic panic as if I was trying to put out a fire. I sat there waiting for more water to fill the tub and began to feel I was losing control of everything in my mind. I felt like I wasn't in control anymore. I didn't know which way was up or down as I stared at the water and thought of laying down completely in it and allowing myself to fall asleep. At this moment I began to cry and fought the thoughts that were entering my mind. I cried out for help and asked my God for help. I knew I couldn't continue alone and if I had any chance of correcting what was happening, I was going to need help. At that moment, I felt this energy lift me from under both of my arms. I found myself standing up in a tub of water and just like that I became aware of where I was and what I had to do next.

I turned off the water, climbed out of the tub, grabbed a towel, and walked into my living room to locate my cell phone. I dialed my best friend, Betty. I just knew I had to ask for help, but I still felt embarrassed asking for it. I remember trying to act like I was just calling her to check in, but she must have heard it in my voice because she quickly said, "What's wrong? You don't sound right." I burst out crying and simply said I needed help. Betty knows me very well and she knew right away I wasn't in my own mind and proceeded to tell me she was jumping in her car to drive across town to my place.

As I waited for Betty's arrival, I sat on the couch crying, wondering what was happening to me. I felt as if I was losing all sense of reality. I also felt the presence of my friend Jaime. To this day I believe it was my friend who lifted me out of the water and whispered into my ear for me to find help and to keep living, but to live *my* life, not the one I was living to satisfy others.

That evening Betty stayed with me until another friend, Ricardo, showed up and spent the night to keep me company. The next morning, he was scheduled to fly out town, so I offered to drop him off at the airport. Upon returning to my home, I was feeling a bit better and figured I would tackle some work and try to focus. About an hour into my work schedule, I began to get the same heat sensation I had the previous day. I recognized this and became cautious about it escalating, but I quickly found out it wasn't something I had complete control of. I started to feel confused and lost. This is when I decided to reach out to a friend back in Texas who has known me for a very long time and would be comforting to talk to and hopefully be able to shed light on what I was going through. My friend quickly instructed me to contact my insurance hotline and speak with a nurse because he thought it might be a good idea for me to seek medical help. I took his advice and hung up and called my insurance provider. The nurse I spoke with was very understanding, caring, and helpful. She worked with me to locate my niece who lived nearby and get her to drive over to my place and take me to the hospital. The nurse even went as far as calling the hospital and having me preadmitted so that I would get in as soon as I arrived at the hospital.

I ended up admitting myself on a voluntary psychiatric hold for 3 days. During this hold I was able to take time out to think and discuss what happened and why. All this led to more fulfilling therapy sessions with my therapist for the rest of the year. In 2013 I was finally able to accept my sexuality and begin the coming out process. It wasn't easy, but then again, unraveling 40 years of suppressed feelings such as shame, self-hate, confusion, and many more would take some time and much effort.

As I wrote this chapter, I revisited the events that transpired during this time of my life, and I'm relieved to see that I made it through. That period was so important for me and reshaped the rest of my life. It's exhausting pretending to be someone else and waking up every day wondering who I was supposed to be just to get through the day.

I'm proud of myself for recognizing that I needed help and for working to find that help. Not only seeking out my therapist but swallowing my pride and admitting myself into the hospital when I thought I was losing it all, but really wasn't.

As the kind doctor and nurse told me, *"You've just exited off the highway of life into a rest stop to rest; you'll soon be back on that highway continuing your journey."*

Self-Portrait (Los Angeles 2020)

19

Being Authentic

When I was touring constantly, my friend Betty had a nickname for me; it was "the traveling mattress," and it was for all the wrong reasons. It wasn't because I moved from hotel to hotel, city to city, but because I was having minute relationships with girls and guys (she didn't know about the guys) that I met in many of the cities I visited. She was my sounding board (she still is). I would ring her up to pour my woes about finding love and the emptiness I felt after these minute relationships. I even called her when I took the walk of shame from a woman's hotel room down the dark hotel hallway, passing the housekeepers (trying to make myself invisible to them because of shame), as I made my way to the elevator to get back to my car and head home. During this time in my life, I was living in the moment without any worry of the future and not investing in a relationship for when I would eventually come off the road. I was living the life of a globetrotting bachelor, living two lives—the straight man and the closeted gay man—and in the end, I still found myself feeling lonely.

I know relationships are hard and although I really haven't been in many long-term ones, I have had quite a few short ones. Well, romantic ones at least. There are of course work and friendship relationships we must also consider when analyzing experiences with relationships. I often find myself looking back at the various relationships I've had throughout my life and question if I handled them right; if I was the good boyfriend, friend, colleague. I do this because in my older years I have found myself alone with a deep feeling of loneliness and I can't help but wonder. How did I end up like this? Maybe because I wasn't living my authentic life. I wasn't just being me. I wasn't giving people the opportunity to really get to know the real me because I was too busy playing a role.

In 2013 after those many therapy sessions, I finally admitted and announced to myself, with the help of my amazing therapist Lauren, I AM GAY! My long journey to living my authentic life was about to begin.

Coming out didn't fix everything. It's not like putting on a new outfit and bang, I walk around being my authentic self and all is fine in the world. I deal with 40-plus years of suppressed feelings and emotions and I must work through all that to get to the authentic me and really find out what it is I want/like in life and in a partner.

The struggle of unraveling years of shame, self-hate, and wanting to be accepted didn't make dating men any easier. It got in the way a lot. For example, I began dating this guy, let's call him Bob. We met on one of the dating apps, and he was great! He was funny, intelligent, caring, thoughtful, and very attractive! Score right? Well, it could have been, but I messed it up. During our short courtship I made him feel horrible because I was too concerned with what others would think when they saw us. It caused a lot of arguments and even though he continued to show kindness and care for me, I wouldn't let go of what others thought. To my slight defense I was a newly minted out gay man. I was still not used to being in public with another guy in a romantic sense. Not that we were sharing affection in public (we never did), but because in my mind we were on a date, and I had it in my head that everyone knew it and would judge us. I mean, c'mon, guys hang out all the time and it's just guys hanging out. Why couldn't I just feel that? Well, I didn't and eventually our relationship ended. He deserved something more and at that time I couldn't provide that to him. He eventually met another guy and they married, and we are still very close friends.

I looked up what "authentic" really means and here is how the Merriam-Webster Dictionary defines it:

a. Worthy of acceptance or belief as conforming to or based on fact.
b. True to one's own personality, spirit, or character.[1]

Sometimes I think, *what prevents me from being authentic? Is it fear or shame?* Society is so judgmental toward those who don't fit into its little box of correctness. I'm talking about allowing yourself to love those you want, expressing yourself as you feel you are inside, accepting yourself and believing you are enough! I often remind myself to quit trying to be the person that already exists and be the person I was born to be.

What if all great innovators of the past decided to conform to being someone else or who society thought they should be? That person might not have gone on to be the great innovator that they would become, and they wouldn't contribute to our world as they did. So much talent goes undeveloped because as a youth we are forced to fit into society's little box of correctness.

Just think of what Alan Turing (1912–1954) could have continued to do if he hadn't been criminalized for being gay. His code breaking skills played a pivotal role in intercepting coded German messages that allowed Allies to win several major victories over the Nazis.

Dr. Charles Drew (1904–1950) transformed the field of blood transfusion and the development of a national blood bank and was appointed by the American Red Cross as the director of the first Red Cross blood bank. He was African American.

Both were something society couldn't fully accept at that time, yet they didn't let that stop them.

NOTE

1. Merriam-Webster Online, s.v. "authentic," accessed September 16, 2023, https://www.meriam-webster.com/dictionary/authentic.

Verrazzano-Narrows Bridge (NYC 2016)

20

Fear Driven

*I*t was 2016 and I had just returned from my trip to India. I was in the car headed home from the airport after a 20-plus-hour trip when my phone rang. It was an artist's personal manager who wanted me to take over his artist's tour that started in a few weeks. I should mention that this was after I had taken time off the road to work on myself and come out of the closet. This meant I would be jumping back into tour management as an out gay man and working with an out gay artist.

His management team and I were good friends, and they just happened to be the managers of another artist client of mine. I agreed to take on the tour simply because I really enjoyed working with them and it would be a great opportunity to work with this artist. Plus, we were going to visit a few countries I had not visited and always wanted to—Russia was one of them!

This was a difficult tour for me because I didn't know how to be myself now that I was free to be me. Looking back, I've come to recognize how I struggled to control things that were not in my control simply because I was still trying to control my closet narrative. The artist knew I was out, but I chose not to make it too obvious to everyone and that's probably where I went wrong. Honestly, I was still concerned with what others would think, and since I was working with some old colleagues from previous tours, I was afraid that I wouldn't be seen as strong enough to hold the reigns of the tour, simply because I was gay. Because of this I drove myself crazy worrying about way too many things and trying so hard to control others and things that simply were not mine to control. The artist tried to invite me a few times to go out with him and his dancers, some of whom were gay as well, but I wouldn't allow myself the opportunity to let them see me as a gay person. I guess the embarrassment and fear was still in me. Remember that I had just come out in 2013 and it was 40 plus years of being in the closet I was dealing with! That was a lot to unravel in three years. I found myself at odds with the artist for various reasons but handled them poorly simply because I was trying too hard to overcompensate for what I thought was a lack of strength because I was now a known gay person. I was buying into the stereotypes that society had projected on the LGBTQ+ community for many years. And there I was, trying to be authentic in being me and yet facing all those misinformed projections society slapped on my community and beginning to believe them and question myself.

I had brought friends and colleagues from other tours to help run the tour with me, so I was surrounded by familiar faces, but they knew me as a straight guy, and I still hadn't told any of them of my coming out. Being surrounded by many more gay guys on this tour only made it more difficult for me because I so wanted to associate with them and feel the warmth of community, but I still had strong fears of judgment, shame, and rejection. So, I chose to isolate myself and only on occasion be with my straight friends and continue to project the old closeted me instead of the authentic me.

Over time I became angry and jealous towards my fellow LGBTQ+ colleagues because they were able to be themselves and boy were they having fun. I, on the other hand, just piled on the responsibilities and took a serious approach to everything. I forgot how to live and have fun, and I became miserable.

The tour itself was a logistical challenge and, because I took over at the last minute, there was a lot of catching up I had to do. So that added to the stress I was already carrying.

We finished the tour, and I was exhausted to say the least, but I also felt like a failure. I felt that I had missed a great opportunity to embrace my community and myself and get a feel for what it was to be authentic in this old world of mine, the touring world. I wrapped up the tour and walked away feeling I didn't make new friends and I probably weakened a few old friendships as well. All because of my behavior; the person I was and how I acted wasn't me—either the closeted me or the out me—it was a whole new persona I created out of fear of people finding out my truth, confusion on how to be authentic and not be ashamed of it and wanting to be accepted for who I was and still having the respect of my position. Why do we care so much about what others think?

I learned that I didn't have to act or be a certain way to fit into the role I held. I was in the role I was because of my abilities, skills, and experience, not because I was straight. The proof was staring me right in the face and I failed to see it. The two personal managers that managed the artist were both gay. And they were highly respected, successful, and well-liked by many in the industry. This goes for so many friends and colleagues I've have in the industry that are also gay. What matters is how you treat people, how you carry yourself, and how well you do your work. I allowed myself to buy into a false narrative that was the opposite of who I was as a person. I'll never be able to please everyone, but I will be able to please myself by just living as my authentic self and embracing those who wish to be part of my life and letting go of those who don't. I missed a first opportunity to experience life on the road as an openly gay individual and interact with everyone as my true self. To be able to go out with fellow gay individuals and partake in fun activities and see how it is to live openly gay. I allowed fear to pull me back into the closet when I had others offering their hand to lead me out.

21

The Go-Go's

I started working with The Go-Go's in 2005 after receiving a call from their then-manager Bradford. When I was presented the opportunity, my mind quickly went back in time to my high school car washes and all my friends and I dancing to their songs as we washed cars. Back then I never thought I would be taking such a call. I of course said yes, and that journey lasted for 17 years, both as a tour manager then as a personal manger.

When I took over personal management duties, I presented a list of goals I was aiming to achieve under my tenure as manager.

They were as follows:

1. Take them to Europe
2. Produce a documentary about them
3. Book a big US tour
4. Book a UK tour
5. Increase their revenue
6. Get nominated to the Rock and Roll Hall of Fame

I was able to accomplish all of these goals. The two proudest moments of my tenure as their manager were producing the documentary about their lives (which won two Critics' Choice Awards), and being nominated & inducted into the Rock and Roll Hall of Fame.

When I took on the role of personal manager, I was transitioning from having been in tour management for 20-plus years. I brought with me years of experience in management of people, situations, logistics, finance, and in building relationships with vendors, promoters, agents, and many other folks along the way. But was I ready to make the move? At first, I questioned if I could do the job. I didn't know what it took to be a personal manager or what I was supposed to do. I soon found out what it took and realized I had already been doing much of that work as a tour manager, so I just did what I've always done, lean on those I trusted and respected to help me along the way, just like before.

PRODUCING THE DOCUMENTARY

I had been talking to the band about a documentary for many years and I felt very passionate about it and its success, so I wanted to find a producing team that shared those same feelings.

When I received the green light from the band to begin shopping around the idea of the documentary and finding a team to produce it, I jumped at the opportunity and put out various feelers in the circles I had in TV/film production. Gerri, the band's business manager, was helpful in getting me started by introducing me to Wally (he was involved with various IP (Intellectual Property) projects on various levels and would be helpful in making connections). One of my first stops to pitch the idea was to a company that had done many reality projects and was in the process of doing a docu-series for an iconic Latin music artist. I thought that was a great start. Unfortunately, I felt they didn't have the same enthusiasm for the project as I did or the vision to bring it to life. So, we moved on.

Our next stop was talking with producers Corey and Trevor. They both had the right combination of experience, enthusiasm, and determination to help bring this to life.

Once it was agreed that Corey and Trevor were the ones to give it a try, we got the shopping agreement in place for them to begin talking about it in industry circles and working to secure investors and a director. I knew of Alison (the director) and had watched the Eagles documentary she directed and loved it and just had the feeling she was the right one for the project. I felt it was going to take a director that would make the band feel comfortable and safe for them to open up to and be honest during their interviews. This was the key to getting the audience to support it. I mentioned it to Corey and Trevor, and they liked the idea. It helped that Trevor had a friend who had worked with Alison and would be able to make the introduction. When I finally spoke with Alison on the phone, it solidified my feelings that she was the one for the project. She was tentatively onboard; we just needed the band to approve her.

At the same time all this was happening we were handed a major win when Polygram (the TV/film division of Universal Music Group) stepped up to finance the entire project! This was huge! We had the money, director, producers, and story—all we needed was the artists to agree to do it. This is the reverse of the way most projects get done in Hollywood; it's usually the money that is the hardest to secure!

Now all eyes were on me. My abilities to present all this to the band and get them to commit to the project were on the table. This endeavor would take almost a year. It would take many discussions with the band individually and as a whole to get a full majority agreement to do this. I felt strongly that the project wouldn't work without all the members participating. It just wouldn't work. The band had obvious concerns, such as how it would represent them, what exactly was going to be discussed, and the trust of the director in presenting an honest and good story. These were all valid concerns. They didn't want a sensational trash-talking piece, and neither did I.

There were times when I had three yeses and two no's, then three no's and two yeses, and the combination jumped around all the time. I was pulling my hair out and watching my anxiety and frustration take a toll on me. Once I even hit a majority "no" from them and I was crushed. I felt strongly about the project—their story needed to be told in their own words and cemented for generations to come. They were trailblazers, pioneers, and women in an industry heavily run and guarded by men, and they succeeded! I also identified that it would be the launching pad for many things to come, including a nomination to be inducted into the Rock and Roll Hall of Fame.

I didn't give up. I gave it time to breathe and gave them time to rethink everything. During this time, we were in the process of debuting their Broadway show so we were going to have to go to New York City to announce it and do a performance. I took this opportunity to have Corey and Trevor meet us in New York City, and, knowing that Alison lived on the East Coast, it made perfect sense to have her meet the band face-to-face so they could feel comfortable and hopefully sign off on the project. I arranged for a private dinner to take place with the band and Alison so that the creatives could have time to get to know each other and allow Alison to present her vision for the film. Nothing like breaking bread to make all parties relax and feel comfortable. Well, it worked! They agreed to have Alison direct the film and the film was back on track.

In the following weeks, there were a lot of legalities that needed to be sorted out between all parties and that was a journey itself. But I'll spare you the details; there are just too many, where to, as to, herein and so forth to share.

The project was agreed to, and the funding was in place! Soon the scheduling of interviews began. The production team took care of logistics and the scheduling of all interviews. I oversaw the band's time commitments for this, among various other advisory discussions regarding the film as executive producer. The various interviews took about six months to film and the editing took about another nine months. In all, the project took about two years before public eyes saw it.

We debuted it at the Sundance Film Festival in January 2020. Having my film debut at Sundance is a feeling no other can replicate. It was mind blowing to know that I was a producer on a film about an iconic band that I managed, and it was debuting at Sundance Film Festival!

After weeks of planning and coordinating, the time came to fly to Park City, Utah, for the big reveal. Getting there was a challenge because flights sold out fast and the pickings were minimal by the time we locked everything in. Our flight there was filled with various Sundance participants, including directors, producers, artists, journalists, executives, and so on. They were all going there for the film festival. It felt like a party bus in the air. I could feel the excitement all around. Everyone was talking to each other like they knew each other—it was the shared connection of going to Sundance, presenting a film, and such. Behind me sat Ron Howard and his producers that were debuting their film as well. I was traveling with two band members and when we landed in Park City, Utah, I turned around and introduced myself to Ron. He was so cool and easy going. He mentioned that he had heard the buzz about our film, and it blew me away to hear him say this. He recognized Belinda who was seated in front me and as we all stood there waiting to exit our rows, they talked about a previous project they worked on, and he mentioned again about the buzz he heard and congratulated us. Everyone was saying hi to each other and mentioning their films and congratulating each other and laughing and just sharing in the surreal moment it was.

The film was well received by audiences and reviewers alike. There was not one single bad review ever presented to me by our amazing PR team and the journalists that conducted the many band interviews were over the moon at the story. The film was a hit as I had suspected, and I felt pretty good because their story was being told in their own words and the record was being set straight for future generations. The film was awarded two Critics' Choice Awards! One for Best Music Documentary and the other for Most Compelling Living Subject of a Documentary.

I feel honored and proud to have been an executive producer of this film, nurturing it from an idea to become a completed film premiering at the Sundance Film Festival. None of my childhood dreams mentioned this happening.

It was a long process to premier the film at Sundance. There were many ups and downs along the way, and many stressful moments. There were times when the imposter syndrome was strong and caused me to have doubt in myself and my abilities. My passion and strong beliefs for the project kept me moving forward. I would continually tell myself that I wouldn't be where I was if it wasn't for my experience. I would dig deep into my past on how I handled similar situations and approached them with the knowledge I had acquired. My respect for patience grew, as did my resilience throughout the entire process of the project and I'm grateful for that because I know it will serve me well in the future.

The Go-Go's & Art @ Rock & Roll Hall of Fame Induction Ceremony (Cleveland 2021)
Photo Credit: Arnold Neimanis

Art walks the Go-Go's to the stage at Rock & Roll Hall of Fame Induction Ceremony (Clevland 2021)
Photo Credit: Arnold Neimanis

Belinda Carlisle on tour bus @ The Stone Pony (NJ 2016)

22

All That Glitters Isn't Gold

Recently I was listening to a voice message my friend Natalie from Australia left me. In the message she reminded me that the life I sometimes think of as ordinary is viewed as extraordinary by many people, simply because I'm dealing with the stars they idolize. To some degree it's just a "the grass is always greener on the other side" situation. My job can be glamorous at times, but honestly, it's a lot less glamorous than you think.

For example, while in Spain on tour, the shows were taking place in bullrings with thousands of fans. Although bullrings weren't built to accommodate productions like concerts, they do have the space to hold the capacity of fans we needed, so we had to get creative with the space to make it work. We had to find dressing rooms for the artist, band, dancers, and so on. We also needed to find a space for catering to be served for all those traveling with the production and then we needed to find space to set up the offices for production, management, and so on. On this one occasion we had to set up the production office in the area where the bull is hung up after it's been killed, so we had to wait for workers to wash the blood away and disinfect the area thoroughly before we could inhabit it. When we did, all we could smell was the bleach they used to disinfect it with. How's that for glamorous and luxurious?

I've taken friends/family backstage and once the golden curtain is pulled back, they are left surprised to find out the lack luster behind-the-scenes. I've heard it many times, "This is it? This is where you spend most of your time?" You see, the fun and excitement are out front where the fans are watching the show, not backstage. From backstage you sometimes can't hear the music clearly, you can't see the artist's face or the lights or the video screens, and so on. Backstage is where the engine is working, keeping the show moving from city to city, like an engine under the hood of a fancy, shiny car.

It takes a lot of dedication doing what I do, and a lot of long hours. Yes, I traveled around the world, but it wasn't like I was sightseeing every day in every city I was in. Many times, while on tour, we roll into a city just like the wind, passing by. The hours are long and, when on tour, I'm surrounded by many amazing colleagues who are also working long hours covering their area of responsibility. I do like to think the beauty of my job is that my office view changes daily, and I could have a tough day in Paris then a great day in London; it's never mundane.

I recognize the amazing career I've been lucky to have and the amazing things it's afforded me, but I also recognize the sacrifices I've had to make to be in this position. Traveling as much as I have doesn't leave much time to be home and nurture a relationship; it's not easy. And for me it's been noticeably absent. Of course, I've had relationships, but they have been minute ones. I've fallen in love in Australia, Spain, New York, St. Louis—and yet I sit here writing my book a single man. All things come with a cost, nothing is free, remember that.

Aside from that, there are also the mental challenges that develop from a world like mine. Always on the move, deadlines every other day that must happen (the shows), juggling all sorts of personalities, keeping them together to accomplish the goal or keeping them apart; whatever it takes. I play therapist, parent, boss, friend, educator, adviser, and so on. When I'm touring, I'm surrounded by a lot of people daily, including the crew/staff of the tour, the thousands of fans at shows, plus all the venue staff as well. It goes on day in and day out for however long the tour is, three months or more sometimes.

Then one day I go home for some time to regroup. I arrive to an empty apartment, and I'm jolted to remember I'm alone and don't have a partner and all that comes with that. To those that do have partners and family, they return to a system that has its established rhythm and they try hard to not interrupt the flow and hopefully jump in and be a part of it without disrupting it too much. That's not easy, but I'm sure they also get hit with the jolt of what they have missed in their loved one's lives. The birthdays, special events—it's the price to pay for the constant traveling we do. A friend once told me, "Yes, I'm surrounded by my wonderful wife and kids, but I still feel alone."

When a celebrity is at a certain highly recognizable level, everyday life can be very challenging. Some artists can't just walk out of their hotel room and take a walk without getting mobbed by fans. They spend a great deal of time in their rooms, and this can bring on loneliness, isolation, depression, anxiety, and many other things. I've seen it.

I've even worked with one artist that had stage fright and was constantly working on overcoming it. Looking at them I could see this "bigger than life" persona, the image that has been honed and crafted, but what's inside was something else. The artist the public sees is not the artist I saw. I saw the person who worried about being liked, worried about finances, love, being in the closet, depressed . . . struggling with life in general. As the saying goes, "all that glitters isn't gold," and that couldn't be truer here.

Touring is a big endeavor; it takes a lot of people behind the scenes to make it happen. And all these people must get paid, housed, transported, fed, and so on. All this is generated by the artist; just imagine the weight of that responsibility. The actions of the artist controls if all these people will have jobs to be able to support their families. If the artist cuts a tour short just because they want to, all these people are out of jobs. And post the Covid-19 pandemic, the costs of putting on a tour have skyrocketed, making it more challenging to make it financially viable for many.

As a manager, I'm tasked at making things happen in the career/lives of my artist. Sometimes it's not music related! It takes diplomacy, strategy, foresight, confidence, and a strong skin because I'll get blamed for everything that goes wrong and not often recognized when they do go right. It's just part of the job—not everyone can do it, but it's pretty rewarding when the projects are completed. I feel like I've brought music to the masses; I've left my fingerprint on something that someday in the distant future someone will revisit and hopefully enjoy.

Paddyism

"The performance is continuous, 24 hours a day at specified intervals we let in the audience. Somewhere 24 hours a day when you are on tour a wheel is rolling, a roadie is working or somebody is in a hotel room writing a song, something is going on, contributing to the eventual performance that occurs in those very rare moments in terms of the whole-time fabric of the tour in which the audience is there and the lights are on."

23

Patrick "Paddy" Stansfield

Patrick Stansfield was my mentor, friend, father figure, and boss. And he spent his entire life traveling around the globe with his clients—rock stars.

Because of this, Paddy (as we called him) was always away from home. And at home he had his two daughters who he had to provide for. I came into Paddy's life when his daughters were already teenagers. I saw what he had to deal with as a father from a distance. Sure, he provided a comfortable living for them (he had a nice large home that came with all the comforts anyone can ask for and more). But the one thing missing was his presence.

That's what roadies deal with, being absent in a relationship. Although we try to call and ensure things are provided, we still miss out on a great deal.

Paddy was a wordsmith: he had great use of the English language. He was well read and had a photographic memory. He could describe at great lengths the many hotels he had stayed in, right down to the carpet design that was in the room. He was also a man of details; he paid attention to details and sometimes would personally handle things down to the smallest aspect.

He was raised a catholic and although he didn't practice his religion, he was still true to it until the end. I would know, I went and asked the priest at my church to administer him his last rights. He was particular about this, and I made sure he got his wish granted—again, it was the details.

Paddy came from Cleveland and then moved to San Francisco and started working with Bill Graham, the great promoter and probably the man that put the concert world on the map and the wheels under concert touring. Paddy worked with him for a long time, then he branched out on his own to become a world-renowned tour director, production manager, producer, and all-around builder of careers and productions.

I first met him through Tom Mooney, my first tour manager (who I've mentioned in this book as the man who gave me my first job in this music industry). They were best friends and colleagues. While working for Tom in his office, one of my duties was to answer the calls and field them as instructed. I recall Tom telling me that if a Patrick Stansfield called, I was NOT to have any small talk with him and was to patch him through immediately or if he was out, I would inform him Tom would call him back shortly. I didn't know who Patrick was yet and just thought he was probably not a good person and so I made sure to follow Tom's instructions.

One day Patrick did call and this friendly voice on the other end simply asked to speak with Tom and politely introduced himself and I politely asked him to hold so I could see if Tom was available and then he said, "Oh, are you Arthur?" I corrected him and said I was Arturo. (I don't like being called Arthur; I've only allowed a handful of people call me Arthur, despite me not liking that name, and Patrick made it to the top of the list over the years.) He then said, "Oh, you are the person I'm not supposed to talk to. Tom is afraid I'm going to steal you from him." He laughed and said, "I'll wait for you to connect me. I don't want to get you in trouble." I put him on hold and informed Tom that Patrick was on the line and he quickly reminded me that I wasn't supposed to have any small talk with him and to patch him through to his line. I did so and waited for Tom to pick up, then I hung up.

Later that day, Tom shared with me the reason why he didn't want me to talk to Patrick. It was just a joke. He just didn't want Patrick to smooth talk me into jumping ship and going to work for him. Tom wanted me to stick with him because he really needed my help. I told him, "Don't worry, I'm not like that. I'm loyal to my word." I would later find out that one of the reasons why I was so welcomed into that elite group of individuals (Tom Mooney, Doug Pope, and Patrick Stansfield) was because of that loyalty. They valued that to the heavens, and this was one of the many lessons they taught me about the industry and doing business in the industry.

After the tour with Tom, he informed me that Patrick was going to call me and offer me a job because he needed my help with hotels on the current tour he was working on. I was preparing to go home to El Paso to visit family; I wanted to share with my mom the amazing stories and experience I had just had. Although I did have an amazing time on tour, it was also a challenging time, and I wasn't sold on making it my career and simply thought it was a great experience. Later that day, Patrick called me, and he did offer me a job as Tom had mentioned, but I didn't accept it and left the next day to visit my family.

The next day while in El Paso, Tom called me and was furious with me and asked me why I didn't take the job and if I had any idea what I was passing up. I explained my reasons to Tom, but he then proceeded to put things into perspective regarding the last tour and how different other tours would be. He explained that this tour was just a one-off situation and that I should reconsider before the offer went away. He knew firsthand that Patrick was still willing to give me the job if I called back and accepted. I told Tom I would give it more thought and would decide the next day. My first tour and first job in the music industry wasn't all I thought it would be. I quickly got a taste of what divas are and the world around them and I didn't like it. But I now know Tom was right; other tours and artist have been different and for the better!

After I got off the phone with Tom, I called the only person I knew to call. She was a recent friend I made on the tour and had been working in the industry for a while and knew all the players. I called her and asked her if she knew who Patrick Stansfield was, there was a pause followed by a loud "Hell Yeah!" and she quickly asked me why and how I heard of him and why I was asking. I told her what had transpired, and she proceeded to inform me of how important a man Patrick was in the industry and how lucky I was to have a person of his stature reach out to me and so early in my new touring career. After a long talk with her, I called Tom back to tell him I was taking the job and he was happy and told me not to waste a minute and to call Patrick immediately. I called Patrick and accepted the job to work on the Michael Crawford tour. He informed me that he was going to work out getting me to Atlanta, GA, to join up with the tour since it had already started.

From then on, I became an associate of Patrick Stansfield & Associates and joined the ranks of a few great people that he mentored throughout his life. I was fortunate to elevate our relationship beyond mentor. He was my second father in my life, and he later told me as he was near the end of his life that I was the son he never had.

Patrick was a man that helped many people with their careers and helped many people build businesses that to this date are leaders in the industry of live event production. He worked with many of the great artist of our times, including Neil Diamond for over 25 years, and many others like Barbra Streisand, Santana, the Rolling Stones, Bob Dylan, Tina Turner, Paul Simon, and even The Pope, plus many more. He was not a perfect person, and he knew it. He would remind me of this often and would tell me to take the good and leave the bad behind, referring to the lessons he dispensed via his many stories he shared with me and examples of how he solved situations he encountered throughout his life and career.

Throughout our long friendship I've spent many of days and nights working alongside him and just hanging out chatting. As I've said before, he was more than a mentor to me. Early in our relationship as I was still learning the ropes of the business and new to working in his office, he invited me over to his home for Thanksgiving dinner. Upon arriving to his home, I found myself in the company (as I would find out later in my career) of many important people in the industry that just happened to be his close friends. I couldn't believe that I was there and often wondered why I was singled out and invited. I thought to myself, *Do I belong here? Why am I here?* Early on Paddy saw something in me and believed in me, although I didn't realize it then. I recall his ex-wife and girlfriend were present. Quite frankly, I was just impressed that he could have these women in the same room at the same time. I guess it was still foreign to me that you could remain friends with ex-lovers. The next day I asked Paddy about this, and I remember him telling me that just because he wasn't married to them anymore didn't mean he didn't still like them or that he didn't once before. He said, "Arthur, life is too short for you to go through life like that. Just remember the good times and carry that with you as you move on."

Later in life Paddy met his fourth and final wife, Claudia. She was just wonderful, full of life, caring, and spunky! To this date she is still a dear friend of mine and I've often gone to her for guidance as I did with Paddy. I recall seeing them together and the love and joy they shared was very present for all to see. I used to tell them that they were two teenagers in love, and they really were.

We were working on the premiere of *The Hobbit: The Desolation of Smaug* when Paddy's health began to decline. It would be the last project we would work on together. Paddy was the reason why we secured the job; he won the clients over with his charm and extensive knowledge of *The Hobbit*'s original book and the actual experience that was set up in New Zealand, and since the client was the New Zealand tourism board, it was perfect!

I had high respect and admiration for Paddy, and he knew it. He meant the world to me, he still does. I took time to be by his side throughout his illness and helped him and Claudia in any way I could. I would drive him to doctors' appointments, organize his medication, run errands, and just hang out and keep him company. It was hard to see him go through everything he went through, but he would tell me, "Arthur, this is the price I must pay for all the bad decisions I made throughout my life." Paddy loved his friends and cherished his relationships; he would call or send emails to people all over the world to chat and catch up. To this date, I still have a voicemail he once left me just to tell me that he felt remiss because he hadn't paid much attention to his friends and just wanted me to know how much I meant to him. I listen to it often just to hear his voice.

One of the last calls I received from him was very late in the evening. He couldn't sleep, and his caretaker had stepped away. He wanted me to come over and be with him. He felt alone and just wanted some company. I regret not doing so just because it was too late, but I told him I'd see him first thing in the morning. I did see him the next morning, but that week his health declined tremendously and within a week he passed. I think of this from time to time, what it would have meant to him for me to go over and keep him company during this time of need. We have all been there when we just need a friend to keep us company, but I think he saw the end was near and was afraid as it got closer. I didn't know this at the time and looking back I wish I had just gone over and sat with him.

I was at the hospital for days as the inevitable time drew closer and closer. I witnessed a parade of visitors come by to say hi and pay him a visit. The hospital staff was amazing in allowing us the overwhelming number of visitors to pass through. I recall one nurse telling me, "Wow, who is he? He is loved by so many."

I smiled and simply said, "Yes, he is. He touched many lives during his time here."

The last time I saw him, I was sitting in his room with Claudia, his daughter, and my dear friend Brian (another protégée of Paddy's), and as the late evening went into the early morning, Brian and I finally decided to retreat to our homes for a short rest as we waited for Paddy to take his last breath. I didn't want to leave, but Claudia insisted we leave to get some rest. I leaned over and whispered to him, "Let go, go on and be with your parents and our friend Tom," and I also told him if he did go, to stop by my place and let me know. At around 5:30 a.m. I felt a presence in my dark bedroom that woke me up and in that moment my phone rang. It was Claudia, letting me know that he had just passed. I told her, "I know, he stopped by to say good-bye."

Paddyism

"People are more important than money."

Patrick & Art at Casa Vega Restaurant (Los Angeles 2009)

24

Investing in Yourself

L et me take you on a short trip with me to when I decided to attend a silent meditation retreat for seven days.

I had been practicing silent meditation for about a year and half and enjoying it. As I mentioned earlier, I first got into mediation with the help of k.d. lang when I was her tour manager. She taught me two mantras to chant along with my mala beads that I had brought back from India. I had been trying to get into meditation before this, but it wouldn't stick. I would be on and off a lot. k.d. taught me how to focus by chanting the mantras and feeling the vibrations, and this worked! I did this for a while but then stopped for a bit before I decided to try silent meditation. I researched and tried various apps on my phone and finally found one that stuck! It was the Ten Percent Happier app. Yup, just like the book that was written by Dan Harris, the former ABC News anchor. His approach is very practical, and he brings the practice of meditation off the cushion and incorporates it into everyday life. The instructors he has enlisted to help with the teachings are amazing and the top instructors of meditation in the United States. I quickly found my favorite instructors and would listen to a great deal of their meditations and teachings. The reason I mention all this is because this is what got me focused on investing in myself.

I was nearing my end of a consulting job for my friend's travel company and had just gone through a challenging time making the documentary. My life was a mess (in my opinion). I was concerning myself deeply about my future and was fixated on what I was going to do after this or that and what if the documentary didn't do well and how was I going to make a living—contrary to popular belief, a producer of documentaries doesn't make a ton of money and I certainly did not. Anyways, my stress and anxiety were getting the best of me, fast. I didn't want to be consulting anymore, there wasn't any more I could bring to the company that would improve on what I had already done, and I was getting ready to end my commitment, but was afraid to tell my friend.

In past sessions with my therapist, Monica, we had explored the idea of me finding a retreat to go to for a weekend and see if that could help with my trauma from my past and all the anxiety I was currently experiencing.

One day I was driving to the office with the intention to tell my friend and end my commitment, but my mind would not stop racing with all these thoughts of life, the future, the documentary, my lack of a relationship, my loneliness, and everything else I was dealing with. As I was driving, I called my best friend and told him what was going on as I burst into tears trying to get the words out all while driving down the winding road of Laurel Canyon. He strongly suggested

I call my therapist, which I did. She was finishing up something but said she would call me in ten minutes once she was done. When she called back, I had already parked along the side of the road down the street from the office to gather myself. I knew I couldn't face anyone. I felt as if I was losing control of my life and my thoughts, and I was afraid. She talked me through my panic attack, and we came to the firm decision that I would find a retreat immediately and enroll in it.

When I finally went home, I was focused on finding a retreat. I began researching various retreats and seeing which one would work for me. This is when I came across Spirit Rock Insight Meditation Center. They were conducting a weeklong LGBTQ+ retreat in a few weeks, and it was being led by one of my favorite instructors from the Ten Percent Happier app. I couldn't believe this; it was meant for me to go there. I didn't waste time working out all the logistics and booking the retreat. But wouldn't you know it, it would take place the same week we were due to announce the premiere of the documentary and I knew it would be a day of press wanting to reach out to the band for a comment, which, as the band's manager, I would need to coordinate. I also knew I couldn't put off attending a retreat much longer for my own mental health. I decided to talk to the other producers and the band about this, and they were all very supportive of me taking the time I needed to attend the retreat. We all knew it wasn't the best timing, but my health was more important. I prepared everything I needed to arrange before I left, and the business manager (Gerri) was prepared to jump into my shoes and coordinate the press requests as they came in.

The retreat took place the week of December 2–9, 2019. The documentary announcement was taking place on December 4, the Wednesday right in the middle of the retreat. On the day I was to travel to the retreat, I woke up to a rainstorm in Los Angeles. Yeah, it hardly rains here and this day it did. Well, as I was getting ready, I received a text that my flight had been cancelled due to the weather. I couldn't believe this. I called the airline, and they were quick to say that they could book me on the next flight the following day, but obviously that wasn't going to work for me. As a very experienced traveler, I knew I could get them to book me out of another airport that was able to handle the weather. After an hour I was able to get them to book me on a flight out of LAX, but I had to rush to get there on time, since that airport is 45 minutes away from my home. I quickly called for a ride and planned to get there as fast humanly possible. Throughout these challenges I was thinking that maybe I shouldn't go. I thought, *Maybe this is a sign that I need to stay and focus on the documentary.* But then I thought, *Maybe this is a test to see how much I want it,* so I jumped in the car and headed for LAX. While in the car, I cancelled my original shuttle from the San Francisco airport to the retreat center (which was in the mountains outside of San Francisco). I booked a new one with my new arrival time. Great! I'd make it in time.

I arrived at LAX, checked in, and then headed to the gate, just to find out my flight had been delayed. *Oh no, not this,* I thought, *boy, someone doesn't want me to go!* But no, I was going, so I just sat there and waited. I did end up flying out at the new scheduled time. I was happy to be on the plane, but knew I was going to arrive late and miss the welcome reception where I would meet all the instructors and my fellow retreaters. I landed and rushed to get my bags and locate my shuttle. I was the only one on the shuttle so that made for an easy ride and my driver was so cool; we had a great conversation the entire hour it took to get to the center.

My driver was very knowledgeable of the retreat because he had driven many people to that same retreat in the years he had worked as a shuttle driver. He was able to give me some insight on the transformation he saw in people going in and coming out. "The transformation of energy was noticeable," as he put it. Along the way he pointed out various key landmarks of San Francisco and the surrounding areas; it made the drive fly by and took my mind off everything.

Once I arrived, I noticed the time and realized I did miss the arrival reception and was close to the start of the program orientation. I located the main office where we were supposed to check in and they were quick to take me to my room so I could drop my bags and rush over to the orientation. I walked into the big round meditation hall and found about 100 people sitting on meditation cushions getting ready to listen to the instructors. I quickly grabbed a cushion and found a spot and made myself comfortable and took a much-earned breath. I turned to the person beside me and introduced myself as did she.

Then the instructors made their way to the center of the circle where they would conduct the daily lessons and mediations. Anushka was the main instructor and the one from the Ten Percent Happier App. She introduced the rest of the amazing instructors and then began to give us an overview of how the week would transpire. They shared with us all the dos and don'ts and so forth. Then came the time when they pointed out the baskets that were going to be passed around with a paper, pen, and plastic bags. They proceeded to explain that these were for those who still had their cell phones. Everyone was instructed to power down their phones and write their names on the paper and place them both in a bag and drop it into the basket. The cell phones would be retrievable at the end of the retreat when we checked out! I had already turned mine in when I checked in, so I was all set. Oh, did I remember to mention that this was a silent retreat?! Yes, no electronics of any kind were allowed, no computers, cell phones, radios, TVs, Kindles, and so on. No communication was allowed either, meaning no talking, sign language, goo-goo eyes, writing, or reading. The only exceptions were when we would have a group session or when we were talking to the instructor or reading our schedules that were posted daily. And I was going vegetarian for a week, by no choice of my own; that's what they served.

This was going to be my week and at a time when my first film as a producer, a very important one at that, was being announced! I was going to be cut off completely from the outside world for a week. My retreat week consisted of eating, meditating as a group, dharma talks, group sessions, individual meditation time, and many solo walks around the picturesque grounds where wild turkeys and peacocks roamed. There were hiking trails that led up the mountains and streams to sit next to in silence with my own thoughts. It was and has been the most peaceful time I've ever spent on this planet.

The week went by slow; it felt as if within the limits of the compound there was this force field that slowed everything down. I never did find myself thinking of the outside world I left behind. I wasn't thinking of the future and worrying, nor was I thinking of my clients, the film, or anything else. It was amazing at how I was able to disconnect completely.

After the retreat I flew home and decided not to turn my cell phone on until I arrived at my home airport. When I did, I found over 400 emails, 100 texts, and a full voicemail. The pre-retreat me would have panicked, but I didn't panic nor did my anxiety rise. I just knew I would get to them in due time one by one and it was okay.

This retreat taught me that I couldn't control much in my life, and what I could, I must do it with gentleness and patience.

This took place December of 2019. I didn't know it then, but the skills I learned while on this retreat would serve me more immediately than I expected. Just three months after this retreat, the world would enter a crippling period that still affects many to this day. Covid-19 shoved us into isolation for months on end with news of the increasing number of deaths around the world and devastating symptoms it inflicted on its victims. Because of the retreat I was able to deal with everything that was happening and get myself through the pandemic. I strongly believe that if I had not attended the retreat, I wouldn't have survived through the pandemic. Again, it was meant for me to attend the retreat and look after my own well-being and I'm glad I listened to my instincts. I work daily at being mindful of the present.

I remind myself

Yesterday is a memory,
today is happening,
and tomorrow is just a thought.

©2013 Art Cisneros

Girl in Thought (Los Angeles 2013)

25

Trust the Process

*I*n May of 2022, I decided to step away from the industry and take some time to re-evaluate my life and future. The pandemic has caused many people to do this and put more value on the quality of life they are living and focus more on life-work moderation. I needed to be doing something more purposeful and fulfilling. I also wanted to do something more creative.

The desire to write this book had been something that I've had for several years, and I figured that this would be the perfect thing to dive into and finally bring it to reality. I also wanted to invest more time into my photography and advance my creative vision in that area. I was fortunate to be able to take the rest of the year off work and focus on me and my passions, and I would remind myself often, this time it's for me.

I had an idea of what I wanted to write about but didn't have any idea on how to go about it. A while back I did attempt to write a book about my industry, but it wasn't anything worth moving forward so I knew I had to find someone to help me with the process.

This is where Azul (my book coach) came in. But first I need to tell you how I learned about him. I had read the book *I Almost Became Me* by Cory Calvin and found it spoke to me and I zoomed right through it. Because of this I began to follow Cory on social media and would occasionally comment on a few of his posts and he would respond to my comments. One day he posted he was working on his next book, and he mentioned Azul. Curiosity made me click on Azul's tag and I began learning more about him and his coaching program, Authors Who Lead. I reached out to Cory and asked him for an hour of his time to chat with and pick his brain about Azul and his book writing process. We arranged a time to zoom together and talked about various things and hit it off. He encouraged me to reach out to Azul and inquire more about his program and see if it was something that would work for me. This is when I really began to feel that this was the right time to begin writing my book. It just felt right in my gut. I reached out to Azul and, after zooming with him, I realized he was great and the right person to help me get my book out. I was drawn to his backstory and how he approached the process of writing a book—it wasn't about sentence structure, outlines, and so on—it was about the transformative process you go through to bring out the book from within yourself. I knew I was in for a journey and, although I had some fears of what I would encounter regarding my past, I believed it was what I really needed to do to also help myself.

I committed to the program and made a promise to myself just like I did when I first came out to Los Angeles to study at acting school. I was going to be open-minded, bring my walls down, and trust the process. And the process was a bit challenging at first, but the more I opened up to myself, the easier it became. Slowly the book idea began to change and take on a different direction. Three months into the program we still had not done any writing; it was just various exercises that are designed to draw out the book that lives within us. When the time came to write, I was excited to do so but still fearful of what I would write about and how vulnerable I was willing to be. Trusting the process was something I had to keep repeating to myself over and over. Once I began writing, I was blown away at how it flowed. There were days that I would just type nonstop for one hour and other days where the flow was slower and then there were days when I just couldn't find the focus to write anything. I had set a goal of 30 days and an average of 1000 words a day. By the end of the 30 days, I had 35,000 words written. I had my first rough draft!

Throughout this process I've dealt with emotional moments as I reached back into time to bring out the details of past events in my life, all the time trying not to relive them but view them with a more observational approach.

My photography also began to develop more. I found models to work with to create some great images and started feeling more confident about my abilities. I also began to share more of them on social media. The feedback I received was motivating and encouraging. I began to research notable photographers and learn from them and watch courses and interviews. I started working toward sketching out various photography series to be photographed. My creative world was exploding, and I was enjoying it.

By the time October came around, I was in the beginning stages of my first edit and beginning to plan out the timeline and strategy of my book being published. By this time, I was already getting a bit nervous about not working and wondering if I would return to the industry or not and what I would do moving forward. I felt as if my life was already over and I would never find work again. I still didn't have a clear idea of what it was I wanted to do.

The Covid-19 pandemic really did a number on many of us in various ways. Not only did it affect our physical health, but it also had a huge impact on our mental state of being. Many of us were forced to stop our lives for a very long time. I personally lost all my work. My industry stopped completely. It's still recovering and isn't fully back to where it was before the pandemic. Because of this, I went through a rough time. I began to drink heavily. It took every bit of what I had learned during my retreat at the end of 2019 to hold me together. I had my dark moments, but I was able to find the light and not allow myself to fall too deep into them. I'm grateful for the help from my therapist, a couple of my closest friends, three amazing nieces zooming with me, and the laughter I drew from TikTok! One day I woke up and decided to go on a journey in search of a better life. I wanted to find more purpose for my life.

You're reading this book because of my self-discovery. I've been experimenting more with my photography, reading more books, and taking time to just sit in silence and be comfortable with it. Meditating deeper for my mental health and working out more regularly for my physical health, plus much less drinking. I've gone back to volunteering again, taking long walks, and finally feeling good about myself and liking myself more each day.

I don't know where my journey will take me from here, but I know it's not over yet, and that I need to trust the process and remind myself, this time it's for me.

Last Words

KARMA

*"You have a Karmic bank account; there's only deposits
and withdrawals, no loans. You need to treat people
square and pile up a balance by doing simply nice
things. Random acts of kindness that fall within your
capability are never lost in the big sphere of the universe.
Many times, I wonder: How did I come through that?
It could have gone so wrong and yet it went just fine.
We got through it, and no one was hurt, and everybody
was happy with the result. How is it that happened?
The only answer there is, is you looked after your
Karma, and it was there when it was time to make a
withdrawal and the bank of Karma cashed the check."*

Patrick Stansfield

12/19/1943–10/28/2014

Old Man (Berlin 2017)

Acknowledgements

Maya Angelou once said, *"I come as one, but stand as ten thousand."*[1] I couldn't have written this book without the help and support of many in my life.

Thank you: Patrick Stansfield, Tom Mooney, Doug Pope, Edie Siteman, Sal Bonafede, Betty Stafford, Claudia Anderson, Benito Martinez, Ricardo Chavira, Gerri Leonard, Ed McPherson, Lincoln Bandlow, Pierre Langton, Corey Calvin, Jarek Dallos, Natalie (Nat) King, Monica Weil, Lauren Costine, Gary Quinn, my fellow authors from Authors Who Lead Leadership Circle, all my rock star clients, all my touring family and the employees at my local coffee shops where I spent countless hours writing, rewriting, people watching, and of course drinking lots of coffee.

Last but not least, my publishing team that has spent countless hours guiding this book through its many phases to get it to where it is now. Azul Terronez, Amanda Toynbee, Kim Karpowitz, Ann Maynard, Justin Greer, Valene Wood, Deborah Spencer, and Kaitlin Barwick.

NOTE

1. Maya Angelou, "Our Grandmothers," in *And Still I Rise* (Random House, 1978).

About the Author

*A*rturo writes from his homebase of Los Angeles, CA. When he isn't traveling the world with rock stars, he likes to foster rescue dogs and watch reruns of his favorite TV show *M*A*S*H*.

He has worked with artists such as Neil Diamond, Barry Manilow, Huey Lewis & the News, The Go-Go's, Colbie Caillat, David Cook, Adam Lambert, k.d. lang, Ann-Margret, Kylie Minogue, Luis Miguel, David Lee Roth, Barbra Streisand, Jane's Addiction, Blake Lewis, Michael Crawford, Yanni, Tonic, and many others. He also co-executive produced the Go-Go's documentary and has produced many high-profile events.

I would appreciate your feedback on what chapters helped you most and what you would like to see in future books.

If you enjoyed this book and found it helpful, please leave a **review** on Amazon.

Visit me at

WWW.ROCKSTARADJACENT.COM
WWW.PSA-ENTERTAINMENT.COM

where you can sign up for email updates and purchase some of my photographs.

Thank You!